THE IMPACT OF REPARATIONS ON THE POST-WAR FINNISH ECONOMY: AN INPUT-OUTPUT STUDY

KRANNERT GRADUATE SCHOOL,
PURDUE UNIVERSITY
MONOGRAPH SERIES

HORWICH *Money, Capital, and Prices*

JENSEN *The Impact of Reparations on the Post-War Finnish Economy: an Input-Output Study*

THE IMPACT OF REPARATIONS ON THE POST-WAR FINNISH ECONOMY: An Input-Output Study

by

BARTELL C. JENSEN
Associate Professor of Economics
Utah State University

1966
RICHARD D. IRWIN, INC.
Homewood, Illinois

First Printing, October, 1966

Library of Congress Catalog Card No. 66-24608

Printed in the United States of America

PREFACE

The position occupied by Finland in the post-war era was due to the provisions of the Moscow Armistice concluded in September 1944 which imposed upon the Finnish government an obligation to pay a war indemnity to the Soviet Union. As defined by the Armistice, these provisions resulted from Finland's participation in the War as part of the Axis powers.

My purpose in this monograph is to present a brief summary of the events which shaped the Finnish economy in the years following World War II—a period dominated by the imposition of the indemnity—and to show by historical perspective that the form of the Finno-Russian Armistice was a result of the unpleasant experiences of the 1920s, as well as to analyze in terms of an input-output model the impact of the indemnity on the system of mutually interdependent industries.

While the problem of analyzing the impact of this war obligation may easily be posed as one in input-output theory, its solution is not an easy one in detail because relevant input-output matrices were not available. 1956 was the only year for which such a matrix had been compiled for Finland. Since 1952 was the final indemnity year, it was necessary to determine whether Finland's input-output structure remained sufficiently stable to allow the 1956 coefficients to be applied during the payments period.

Thus the general problems of changing input-output coefficients and adjustments on these coefficients to account for change had to be dealt with. An attempt is therefore made in chapters III and IV to derive:

(1) a method of generating price data within an open static input-output framework. These data are then compared with actual price data to determine the stability of the coefficients over time. If prices calculated on the basis of a given set of coefficients do not vary from observed prices which prevailed in some period other than the base period, the coefficients can be considered as invariant. If, on the other hand, the two sets of prices vary widely the coefficients can be considered as varying with time.

(2) a possible method, where structural change has occurred, of transforming the technological relationships of a base year to represent technology as it existed in some year other than the base year.

I wish to acknowledge my indebtedness to Professor Edward Ames, who read the manuscript through its several drafts and offered enumerable suggestions for its improvement. I am indebted to Professors Jay W. Wiley, Duncan M. McDougall, and Rubin Saposnik, who also reviewed the manuscript and offered helpful criticism.

Further, I wish to acknowledge Osmo Forsell and Paavo Grönlund of the Central Bureau of Statistics, Helsinki, Finland, for their assistance in obtaining much of the needed data.

Special appreciation is extended to the Purdue Research Foundation and the Krannert Graduate School of Industrial Administration for the financial assistance which made this monograph possible. Gratitude is also due D. Wynne Thorne, Vice President-Research, Utah State University, for financial assistance during the concluding phase of the work.

Finally, I acknowledge the cooperation of my wife, Arlene, who has patiently and carefully typed several drafts of this monograph.

BARTELL C. JENSEN
Logan, Utah
August, 1966

TABLE OF CONTENTS

1

INTRODUCTION

The recurring tragedy of Finland is that of a marchland state subject to the dual control of Eastern and Western Europe. It lies between the Russian circle of strategic control and the Atlantic circle of economic control. As a political unit it is dependent on Russian policy, though separated from the U.S.S.R. by effective natural barriers. As an economic unit it is oriented to western markets and linked to them by established maritime relations. Finland shows one face to the East, and another to the West. It balances an eastern frontier of conflict and a western frontier of contact. In spite of this, perhaps because of it, Finland has retained an individuality stronger than that of any other eastern marchland state.

The analysis that follows is divided into three parts: First, there is a brief summary of the events which shaped the Finnish economy in the years following World War II, a period dominated by the imposition of reparations resulting from Finland's participation in the war against the Union of Soviet Socialist Republics and the problems encountered in meeting the demands of this indemnity. Second, there is an attempt to show by historical perspective that the form of the Finno-Russian armistice was a result of the unpleasant experience of the 1920s. Third, an input-output approach is applied in an empirical investigation of the interindustrial relationships that existed within the Finnish economy during the period of indemnity payments. More specifically, this approach is made to determine the impact of the reparations on the various interdependent industries or sectors comprising the economy and to indicate the real cost involved in effecting their deliveries.

Postwar Finland and the Armistice

The position of Finland as an independent republic in the postwar era depends upon and is governed by both the Moscow Armistice concluded in September, 1944, and the Treaty of Peace between Finland and the Allied and Associated Powers signed in Paris in 1947. A remarkable achievement lies behind the fact that Finland is still a democratic country. The terms defined by the armistice and subsequent agreements were crippling; few people imagined at the time that Finland would be able to survive the postwar years as an independent state.

The terms set down by the armistice presented three formidable problems to Finland. The first was that of expelling the Germans from her northern provinces. This created much apprehension, for if the Finns had failed to accomplish this unaided, Russian support would have been necessary. This would have meant, it was feared, military occupation, no doubt on a permanent basis. The ensuing campaign against the German troops, even though successful, cost thousands of Finnish casualties plus the ravaging of Arctic Finland, where the Germans in their retreat destroyed bridges, railways, and so on, and burned towns and villages.

A more serious problem was set by the territorial clauses of the 1944 peace settlement in which the bulk of Finnish Karelia was ceded to the Soviet Union. This was the most significant of the four territorial losses. The others were Salla-Kuusamo at the waist of Finland, the Petsamo corridor in the extreme north, and the Porkalla Peninsula. The last of these, commanding the approaches to Helsinki, was leased for 50 years.

These losses directly weakened Finland's political and economic status and brought it more completely within the Russian sphere of control. The country's natural and capital resources were reduced by more than a tenth of the total. Indirect losses such as the decline in accessibility were nearly as great; the loss of Petsamo cut off access to Arctic waters; the annexation of the Karelian province deprived Finland not only of some of her best land but also of one of her most important export harbors, Viipuri, and the Saimaa Canal, channel for the main timber trade. Indeed, before the war the Saimaa Canal made Viipuri the gateway to the most extensive inland waterway system and the largest forest area in the country. Furthermore, the half-million Karelian Finns who migrated to central and western Finland rather than remain under Russian rule had to be resettled and rehabilitated. These territorial losses made the third and most formidable problem, that of reparation demands, more difficult to solve.

Finland's obligation to pay a war indemnity or reparation bill to the Soviet Union was based on Article 11 of the armistice agreement concluded on September 19, 1944, which states:

> Losses caused by Finland to the Soviet Union by military operations and the occupation of Soviet territory will be indemnified by Finland to the Soviet Union to the amount of three hundred million dollars payable over six years in commodities (timber products, paper, cellulose, sea-going and river craft and sundry machinery).[1]

The reparation bill thus defined by the Finno-Russian armistice amounted to $300 million, the dollar being defined as "the American dollar at its gold parity on the date of the signing of the agreement, i.e., $35 per ounce of gold." Further, the bill was to be paid in commodities and the commodities were to be valued at the price level prevailing in 1938, with an

---

[1]Urho Toivola, *The Finland Year Book 1947* (Helsinki: Mercatorin Virjapaino ja Vustannus Oy, 1947), p. 82; also, "Armistice with Finland," *U. S. Department of State Bulletin* (February 18, 1945), Vol. XII, No. 295, pp. 261–62.

increase of 15 percent in the case of capital goods and 10 percent in the case of consumers goods—capital goods consisting of products of the metal industry except for cable products, and consumers goods consisting of cables and products of the woodworking industries. Annual deliveries of reparation commodities were divided into monthly installments and failure to deliver any one of the groups of commodities within the stipulated time period imposed a fine of 5 percent per month on the value of the delayed deliveries. Fines were to be paid either in commodities similar to those which were delayed or in commodities designated by the Soviet Union. Furthermore, a deficiency in one group of commodities could not be compensated by an excess in another. Delays for reasons uncontrolled by the debtor country, such as delayed acquisition of foreign supplies, were in no way to affect the calculation of delay fines.

The real weight of the Russian demands, however, is not realized until the types of commodities demanded are taken into consideration. Only one third of the bill was to be paid in products of the woodworking industries, though these were Finland's staple export and made up over 80 percent of her total exports in prewar years. An additional third of the total bill was to be made up of ships and cables. This may not appear burdensome for a shipbuilding country, but it was, in fact, extremely onerous. Four percent consisted of existing ships, or ships which the Russians presumed still to exist—in some cases they had been sunk during the war, in many cases they needed extensive repairs, and in no case could they be readily spared from the depleted Finnish Merchant Marine. Twenty percent of the bill had to be paid in new ships, largely of types which did not conform to the existing structure and technical knowledge of the Finnish shipbuilding industry and for which it was necessary to set up entirely new yards. As for cables, their manufacture depended largely upon the importation of metal from Sweden. The remaining third of the bill was the most arduous of all. It was to be paid in machines—in locomotives, trucks, cranes, completely equipped plants for the production of cellulose, cardboard, wood pulp, paper, and so forth, and electric motors—machines which Finland had never before manufactured and for which the raw materials, machine tools, plants, and skilled labor were lacking. Altogether more than 60 percent of the reparation goods were to come from the metal and engineering industries, the products of which comprised only 4 percent of Finnish exports in prewar years.

According to the indemnity agreement the specific breakdown of deliveries by types of commodities was as follows: machines and equipment, including installation of completely equipped factories, $100.9 million; new vessels, $60.2 million; paper industry products, $59.0 million; wood industry products, $41.0 million; cable products, $25.0 million; and ships surrendered from the existing merchant marine, $13.9 million.[2]

Reparation Payments

Finland faced the task of footing this bill with a seriously weakened economy. Her manpower had been depleted by the wars of 1939–40 and 1941–44, in which 2 percent of the population had been killed and a larger proportion disabled. The territory of Finland had been reduced by 12 percent, the cultivated area by 9 percent, and forest resources by 12 percent. The loss of Karelia was particularly damaging to Finland's capacity to meet reparation demands. Karelia not only accounted for more than a quarter of the nation's cellulose production, but the new frontier cut both the Saimaa Canal and the Vuoksi River which were essential to the industrial transport and to the generation of electrical power for non-Karelian Finland. Nearly one-third of the developed hydroelectric power was lost when the Vuoksi River was bisected.

Furthermore, under the terms of the armistice, Finland was under obligation to restore to the Soviet Union all property removed from Soviet territory during the war. This stipulation applied not only to original Soviet property but

[2]Jaakko Auer, *Suomen Sotakorvaustoimitukset Neuvostoliitolle* (Porvo., Kirja Paino, 1956), p. 316.

to property which Finland had transported to or constructed on occupied territory and subsequently removed. Where possible, property was to be returned in its original form. For such removals that could not be restored, compensation was to be made by delivery of similar goods valued according to 1938 prices. By May, 1946, when the Soviet Union relieved Finland of any further obligation in this regard, the total value of restitutions, calculated in postwar dollars, amounted to $46.1 million of which $22.1 million represented the return of original Soviet property.

In addition, negotiations at Potsdam gave Russia claim to all German "external assets" located in Finland. These assets were subsequently defined to include not only the German clearing account but all German war materials left in Finland. The Finns were obligated to make deliveries in kind amounting to $17 million under the former account, with the Soviets specifying the goods to be delivered, and to transfer under the latter account all remaining assets ($27.1 million).[3] (Finland, although in the war on the side of the Axis, was the one country in which the Nazis did not pursue the Jewish issue. Quite unlike the situation in other Axis Power countries, property belonging to some 2,000 Jews was left unconfiscated.)[4] Both the transfer of German assets and the restitutions of Soviet property were in addition to the $300 million reparation bill.

Indemnity payments were to commence immediately, granting no period of recovery for an economy suffering from the strains of war. Hostilities continued against the retreating German troops which resulted in almost complete devastation of the northern part of the country. The reconstruction of this area, the repair of war damage elsewhere, and, last but not least, the resettlement and rehabilitation of the displaced population from the territories ceded under the provisions of the armistice treaty were tasks that had to be undertaken im-

[3]Toivola, *op. cit.*, pp. 88–89.

[4]Hannah Arendt, "Eichmann in Jerusalem—IV," *New Yorker*, March 9, 1963, p. 68.

mediately and concurrently with the war reparation drive.

The Finnish war indemnity obligation as determined by the basic agreement was subject to a rigid timing provision; it resembled a clock with a face divided into 72 equal sectors, each sector representing a single month's indemnity payment. It was intended that when the hands had passed around the face the entire reparation obligation would have been paid.

In reality, however, this scheduled balance was not realized. Since the structure of the reparation demands not only failed to conform to the structure of existing industry but also exceeded its productive capacity, the debtor reserved within the limits of a reparation year as long a period as possible to manufacture those reparation items—metal products and machine goods—for which she lacked both the industrial structure and the raw materials, that is, over 60 percent of the first year's scheduled deliveries from the metal industry (not including the transfer of existing ships) were made during the last quarter of the year. Although Finland's metallurgical industry had been expanded through the war years, it was neither large enough nor structurally-suited to meet the reparation demands.

The second factor which broke the balance of the basic agreement was the subsequent alleviations granted by the Soviet Union. On December 31, 1945, the delivery period was extended from six to eight years or to September 19, 1952, and in the summer of 1948 one-half of the outstanding deliveries—goods valued at 73.5 million reparation dollars—was cancelled.[5] The former of these alleviations meant that the annual payments, originally amounting to $50 million, were reduced to about $35.5 million. The latter relief, although of considerable importance to the economy, was concerned principally with products of the forest industry which disappeared from the schedule of deliveries after July, 1948.

The third factor breaking the scheduled balance was the unavoidable delay in deliveries of certain products, primarily

[5]Auer, *op. cit.*, p. 318.

from the metal industry, and the advance deliveries of the more easily manufactured products. Such advance deliveries characterized much of the entire reparation period, especially the first four years following the armistice.

These factors together account for much of the imbalance experienced in the yearly payments of the war indemnity. Instead of six equal annual installments of $50 million as established in the original agreement, annual payments in the immediate postwar years, at a time when the economy was least able to support the indemnity demands, were larger and more difficult to effect than in subsequent years when they were progressively decreased. The development of the war indemnity payments can be conveniently considered in three different stages.

During the first stage—through December 31, 1945—Finland not only met the stipulated obligation of $46.1 million, exclusive of ships from the existing merchant fleet, but succeeded in making certain advance deliveries. The basic groups of commodities constituting these early deliveries were, however, largely from the woodworking industries leaving a serious deficit of metal products and machine goods, primarily of the installation of fully equipped factories for the production of prefabricated houses.[6] This is, in part, attributable to a strike in the Swedish metal industry which delayed the acquisition of basic and semimanufactured materials needed to effect delivery of the delayed items.

During this same period a recurrent deficit of cable products was recorded. Delivery of the stipulated 5,775 tons of bright copper cable, 520 kilometers of power cable, and 361 kilometers of control cable proved to be an impossible task.[7] Not only were local stocks of copper exhausted, but copper production was interrupted while the copper smelter of Finland's leading mining enterprise was relocated.

The debtor, however, through the surrender of tug boats

[6]*Ibid.*, p. 51.
[7]*Ibid.*, p. 60.

and freighters which had been partially built during the war, succeeded in meeting requirements of new ships and in certain cases making advance deliveries. These advance deliveries of new vessels during the initial stage of the indemnity payments largely counterbalanced deficits that occurred in other groups of the metal industry, that is, machines and cable products. However, as a result of provisions in the basic agreement, these advance deliveries were not credited when the delay fines were calculated.

Finland had thus commenced to fulfill her war reparation commitment. But by late 1945 it was apparent that the indemnity demands in their original form far exceeded the capacity of her metallurgical industry. Subsequently, the Soviet Union, even though there was apprehension as to its intentions, eased the reparation burden when in December, 1945, the period of payment was prolonged from six to eight years. The revised agreement, in addition to reducing annual deliveries from $50 to $35.5 million initiated the second stage of the indemnity payments which lasted for the ensuing 30 months—through June, 1948. During this period the indemnity bill amounted to $64.2 and $33.1 million from the metal and woodworking industries respectively.[8]

In order to meet the schedule of demands for metal products and machine goods, the obstacles created by the serious lack of raw materials, plant, machine tools, and skilled labor had to be abolished. Even if Finland's productive resources had remained in every respect the same as they had been prior to the war, the indemnity payments would have required a considerable change in her industrial structure. Industries producing metal products, machine goods, ships, and so on had to be greatly expanded. This necessitated the acquisition of efficient and modern machine tools, semimanufactured goods, and raw materials of foreign origin. By the end of 1948, however, much of the needed increased capacity had been realized. In 1947 the metal industries employed over

[8] *Ibid.*, p. 73.

80,000 workers and in 1952 about 87,500, as compared to 63,600 in 1944. Over the entire reparation period permanent machinery installation in the metal industry increased about 75 percent. It has further been estimated that some 28 billion Finnmarks were invested in the reparation industries. Based on the 1952 rate of exchange, this corresponds to about $121.2 million.[9]

It is significant, however, that even though the revised delivery schedule reduced the annual indemnity load by nearly one-third and much capital expenditure in new factories, plants, shipyards, and the like had taken place, there were still serious difficulties, particularly in the shipbuilding industry. The debtor managed fairly well in meeting the requirements of steel ships, but continual deficits were recorded in the deliveries of wooden vessels, the construction of which required not only the installation of entirely new shipyards, which in many cases were not fully equipped, but skilled labor and heavy timber, which were in short supply. Within the machinery group, delivery deficits again became chronic, while deliveries from the the woodworking industry were deliberately ahead of schedule. Despite stipulations in the basic agreement, the Soviet Union by this time had relieved Finland of part of the payment of delay fines since they had compensated delayed deliveries of machines and ships by substantial advance deliveries of woodworking industry products. This automatically reduced the volume of free exports, but of the two existing alternatives Finland selected the one in which the adverse consequences were considered to be the least.

The third stage of the indemnity payments was inaugurated when the Kremlin announced that as of July 1, 1948, all outstanding deliveries would be reduced by half. This meant a reduction of 73.5 million reparation dollars, almost a quarter of the total demanded. There was, of course, an understandable reason for the timing of this concession. Finland was on the eve of a general election, and the Communist Party wanted to claim the credit for securing Russia's favors.

---

[9]*Ibid.*, p. 322.

According to the amended schedule, Finland had paid two thirds of the bill in the first four years. She had also undertaken much of the capital expenditure necessary for the production of goods to be delivered during the next few years. The reductions, however, were not made evenly over all commodities. They were sweeping in the case of timber products, paper, and cables, but small in that of machinery and industrial equipment, and nil in the case of ships. The last, of course, was precisely the item with which Finland was experiencing the greatest trouble. On the other hand, the reduction in reparation demands for timber products released quantities of these for sale on the commercial export market at a time when demand and prices were soaring. The remaining deliveries—deliveries to be made between 1948 and 1952—were almost exclusively from the metal industry as shown by the following breakdown by groups of commodities: machinery and installation of industrial equipment, $33.2 million; new water craft, $39.3 million; paper and paper products, $0.7 million; sundry deliveries, $0.3 million; totaling $73.5 million.[10] (These, and all other dollar figures presented in this chapter, unless otherwise specified, are "reparation dollars.")

In spite of the increased emphasis on deliveries from the metal industries, the debtor was now able to meet the required deliveries of machinery and industrial equipment, which, prior to 1949, had been perpetually in arrears, and, in some cases, effect advance deliveries. Only during the last quarter of 1950 when a strike in the Finnish metal industry paralyzed the production of both machines and steel vessels were deficits in this area again recorded.

Even though only a few minor obstacles were encountered in the delivery of machine goods in the final stage of the indemnity payments, the Finnish shipyards were under heavy pressure right through the end of the final reparation year. Delivery of 143 new ships valued at $25.8 million had been made during the first four reparation years, but the indemnity program for the remaining four years obligated the debtor for

[10] *Ibid.*, p. 324.

the construction and subsequent delivery of some 371 ships valued at $40.2 million.

The aftermath of the metal industry strike (1950), along with capacity constraints in certain shipyards, resulted in delayed delivery of new vessels through most of the seventh reparation year.

Thus the actual timing of deliveries was noticeably different from the fixed delivery schedule in the original armistice agreement of 1944. In their final form, the war indemnity deliveries consisted of the following: new vessels, $66.0 million; ships from the existing merchant marine (1944), $14.0 million; machine goods and industrial equipment, $70.7 million; cable products, $12.9 million; products of the pulp and paper industries, $34.9 million; and timber and wood products, $28.0 million, or a total of $226.5 million, 72 percent of which came from the metal industries and only 28 percent from the woodworking industries, Finland's staple export in prewar years.[11]

Had the actual amount of the indemnity deliveries, $226.5 million, been divided into eight equal lots over the entire reparation period, the annual payments would have been about $28.3 million, 12.5 percent of the total value. Finland, in fact, delivered in 1945 commodities valued at $57.6 million, or about 25.4 percent of the total eventual delivery. By the end of 1947, over 60 percent of the total reparation bill had been met. Thus the debtor expanded its productive capacity required to effect the reparations by more than would have been necessary had she been permitted to deliver the reparation commodities in annual lots of equal size, or if the modifications of the indemnity obligation had been known by the debtor country at the time expansion was taking place.

Article 6 of the basic agreement, to which reference has been made, obligated Finland to supply "penal deliveries" for lots of commodities that had been delayed from their due dates. The total value of these delay fines would have amounted

---

[11]*Ibid.*, p. 262.

to about $4.6 million for the entire reparation period if the Soviet Union had not been willing to grant further alleviations. Fines that accumulated during the first year of deliveries, $0.3 million, Finland paid in full. During the ensuing three years the Soviet Union abolished the bulk of the delay fines and subsequently fully pardoned Finland of all delay fines. The total value of fines paid by Finland amounted to only $0.8 million, which represented a substantial alleviation by the creditor country.

Pricing of the War Reparation Commodities

The Finno-Russian armistice and subsequent negotiations (the Basic War Reparation Agreement) provided that the value of deliveries was to be determined in United States dollars according to 1938 world market prices, increased by 15 percent in the case of machines, installations, and ships and by 10 percent in the case of consumers goods. Furthermore, the basic agreement specified the individual lots of commodities included in the reparation program and their values, the total of which was $300 million. Since both the price level and the total value for each of the lots of commodities included in the indemnity were supposedly specified, the question of volume should have been a closed issue. In practice, however, the situation with respect to both price and volume was quite different and unsettled. With the exception of deliveries during the first reparation year, the basic agreement, while specifying a set of prices which remained valid for the entire indemnity period, merely established general definitions of the reparation commodities, with the final volume of the individual lots of commodities, as well as the technical details, to be fixed in subsequent annual agreements; that is, exact specifications and amounts of commodities to be delivered were to be set down by the Russians two months before the beginning of each delivery year.

Furthermore, the statement "world market prices prevailing in 1938 increased by certain percentage rates" was in practice extremely vague and misleading. It did not indicate, for example, what kind of "world market prices" were to be applied; whether an average price covering the widest possible base was to be established for each commodity, or whether a single country was considered sufficient for the determination of prices. Even if there had been supplementary stipulations in the agreement making the vague definition "world market price" more exact, determination of the prices of individual and highly varying lots of commodities would not have been an easy task. Only a few of the commodities in the indemnities—certain woodworking industry products and cables—could have been considered "bulk articles" for which world market prices in 1938 were available. Products of the metal industry were not in general "world market commodities." Each item was characterized by special features corresponding to requirements and conditions set down by the Soviet Union. To complicate the price problem even further, certain types of seagoing ships included in the indemnity deliveries, principally wooden vessels, had never before appeared on the Western market.

As early as 1945 it became evident to the debtor country that the seeming twins in the basic agreement, the volume of individual deliveries and the crediting prices, were quite unrelated. In negotiations between Finnish and Soviet war reparation authorities, Finnish spokesman repeatedly asked for a revision to correct the apparent distortions. Soviet authorities admitted that prices with which the debtor had been credited were unrealistic, but that for the most part they were above the pricing base, and that if any revisions were made in the price lists, Finland would be the losing party.

As a result of subsequent calculations by the Finns to determine the relationship between prices with which she had been credited during the first indemnity years and the pricing base, it was admitted that prices for the delivery of steel ships and cable products were in general above the base price, while on the other hand, prices applied to the delivery of machines, installations of completely equipped factories, and wooden vessels were somewhat less than the base price. However, after the Soviet Union modified the indemnity obligation in 1948, Finnish expressions of dissatisfaction were "buried in silence."

Factors Contributing to the Completion of the Indemnity

There appear to be four basic factors that account for Finland's success in fulfilling her war reparation obligation: (1) Finland's own efforts to increase capacity and to meet the demands; (2) the alleviations in the original indemnity program that were granted by the creditor; (3) foreign capital; and (4) advantageous terms of trade during the reparation period.

The first two have already been dealt with; the remaining two will be considered very briefly. The indemnity burden undoubtedly would have been much more severe if Finland had not succeeded in reviving her commercial foreign trade. In 1951 the quantity of goods exported commercially exceeded the 1935 level and was very little below the volume for 1938. Her most important market was the United Kingdom, which absorbed about one third of her total commercial exports. (The Soviet Union, in addition to reparations, absorbed nearly a twelfth and the United States about a fourteenth.) At the same time Finland was increasing her imports, the volume index of which was 55 percent higher in 1951 than in 1935. Furthermore, the terms of trade had shifted in Finland's favor as early as 1945 and by 1951 had reached 157 (1935 = 100). Throughout the entire reparation period Finland's terms of trade remained above the 100 level.[12]

In order to maintain imports necessary for both the indemnity deliveries and for the rebuilding and expansion of the free trade industries, Finland, in the immediate postwar

---

[12]Tilastollinen Päätoimisto, *Tilostokatsauksia,* (Tammikuu 1955) No. 1, XXX–1955; also No. 1–2, SSV-1950, pp. 10–11; also *Bank of Finland, Monthly Bulletin* (1953) Vol. XXVII, Nos. 9–10, p. 28.

years, relied on financial assistance from abroad. Between the end of hostilities and July 31, 1948, Finland had received some $193 million of new long-term foreign loans.[13] Many of these loans, however, were granted for the express purpose of acquiring machinery, appliances, and the necessary requisites for reconstruction and expansion of the basic industries and not for the direct importation of indemnity goods. As will be shown in a later section, after 1948 repayment of loans exceeded the receipt of new loans.

Summary

The payment of the Finnish war reparation to the Soviet Union supplied the creditor country with various kinds of consumer goods, but, more important, also supplied it with such capital goods as machines, completely equipped factories, ships, and so on, the acquisition of which in the world market in the immediate postwar years would have been a slow and costly process. The system in many respects turned out to be very rigid. The due dates of deliveries along with the technical properties of the reparation commodities were specified in full detail. Furthermore, the creditor established a large administrative staff in the debtor country to supervise and effect the smooth flow of payments.

Since the structure of the indemnity demands not only failed to correspond to the structure of Finland's trade and industry but exceeded its productive capacity, the debtor had to greatly expand her industrial potential. This, along with the acute shortage of raw materials and the financial illiquidity of the debtor country during the early stages of the reparation period, seriously disrupted the balance of deliveries. This balance was restored in part after the original schedules had been revised; that is, after the creditor granted a prolongation of the reparation period and reduction of the outstanding indemnity obligation to $226.5 million. After these

[13]Auer, *op. cit.*, p. 339.

alleviations, deliveries, at least for certain periods, were effected with greater precision, which, according to the reparation system of 1944, was to be the guiding principle.

The crediting price system that was applied in the war indemnity had definite weaknesses. Price lists contained in the basic agreement of 1944, which were valid during the entire reparation period, were in many cases quite unrelated to the 1938 price base. Although the contracting parties were aware that distortion existed it was impossible to reach an agreement to effect any changes as long as the final volume of deliveries remained open; with the exception of the first year, the basic agreement specified that the final volumes of individual lots of commodities were to be established in consecutive annual agreements.

Despite the fact that the indemnity was onerous, by calculating the payments as a percent of both net national product and aggregate government expenditure, it appears that the reparations, contrary to conjecture, were not outside the range of economic possibility (Table 1-1, page 18). It is true, however, that the reparation bill, calculated more with regard to the needs of the receiving country than to the capabilities of the delivering country, imposed the heaviest burden at the time when Finland's war-strained economy was at its weakest. If the annual payments had been progressively increased instead of decreased, granting the economy a chance to recover from the ravages of war and to realize the needed industrial expansion, the burden would have been substantially less.

The war reparation posed for the Finns not only the problem of how to meet the indemnity obligation but the question of what was to happen after the completion of payments in September, 1952, to the metal and engineering industries which had been expanded, and in many cases created, to manufacture reparation goods. There was little question of selling their products on Western markets. The new industries, it was feared, would have to be shut down, their capital written off and their skilled workers thrown into unemployment, or they would have to go on producing for the Soviet Union, who as

TABLE 1–1

REPARATION PAYMENTS AS A PERCENT OF NET NATIONAL PRODUCT AND OF AGGREGATE STATE EXPENDITURE

Year	Reparation payments* (mill. mks.)	Net national product at market† prices† (bill. mks.)	War reparations as a percent of net national product	State expenditures‡ (bill. mks.)	Reparations as a percent of state expenditure
1944	265.3	79.61	0.3	38.34	0.7
1945	8,171.5	108.30	7.6	39.01	20.9
1946	8,775.1	181.50	4.8	63.88	13.7
1947	10,404.7	254.08	4.1	75.70	13.7
1948	11,545.6	361.96	3.2	107.27	10.7
1949	12,226.3	382.09	3.2	112.82	10.8
1950	7,845.8	482.79	1.6	127.78	6.1
1951	12,396.4	706.45	1.8	181.21	6.8
1952	8,215.4	716.74	1.1	199.46	4.1

*Statistics received from the Central Statistical Office of Finland, October 10, 1962.
†Tilastollinen Päätoimisto, *Tilostokatsauksia*, (Tammikuu 1955) XXX–1955, No. 1, p. 6.
‡*Bank of Finland, Monthly Bulletin*, 1953, XXVII, Nos. 7–8, pp. 25–28.

the sole buyer would be able to specify her own terms. Some of these doubts, however, were set at rest when the terms of the Finno-Russian trade agreement which had been under negotiation for seven months were announced in June, 1950. Under this agreement Russia undertook to purchase, during the five-year period ending December 31, 1955, basically the same lots of commodities as she had received in reparations during the previous five years. That is, Finland was to continue delivery of industrial and timber-working equipment, cables, vehicles, and vessels, while in turn the Soviet Union was to deliver to Finland wheat, sugar, rye, industrial chemicals, oil, and so on. The value of trade was to amount to $352.8 million each way, with prices to be established on the basis of world prices prevailing at the time.[14]

It stands to reason that if, as a result of a high cost structure, Finnish industry was unable to compete on the Western market, the exchange of goods with the Soviet Union, at world prices, implied a certain deficit which might be interpreted as a disguised reparation payment. It is necessary to recognize, however, that much of Finland's industry was geared to Russian production and as such was not technically suited for Western markets. That is, since the technology of certain industries precluded their entrance into Western markets, it would have been profitable to continue production, even though the Soviet Union represented the sole outlet, only if costs could be maintained sufficiently low—average cost less than or equal to price. It was hoped that on this basis there would be no setting back of the industrial revolution which the reparations demand had accelerated.

[14]*The World Today*, published by Royal Institute of International Affairs, July, 1952, p. 312.

2

REPARATIONS IN A HISTORICAL PERSPECTIVE

In the preceding section the indemnity imposed on Finland by the Soviet Union as a result of Finland's participation in the war as an Axis Power was treated strictly as a domestic problem. Traditionally, and in direct contrast to the domestic approach, indemnity payments have been considered in economic literature as international in nature. That is, the debtor, after raising the indemnity in internal currency, converted payments into external currencies—currencies of the creditor powers. If such a monetary transfer was to be effected in the real sense, an import surplus necessarily followed in the creditor country with a corresponding export surplus in the debtor country.

The theory of transfer, the means of effecting a real capital movement from one country to another, as based on such unprecedented unilateral payments as the Franco-Prussian indemnity of 1871, became the object of debate after World War I when the feasibility of German reparation payments was in question. As a result of the serious maladjustments produced by the war in both the internal economies and the balances of payment of the European countries, the transfer mechanism proved to be ineffective. After a sequence of unfortunate events—breakdown of the London settlement of 1921, French invasion of the Ruhr, hyperinflation in Germany as well as other parts of Europe, and complete destruction of the German currency, along with the final breakdown in the Great Depression—reparation payments were finally cancelled.

With this background clearly in view, the victorious powers at the conclusion of the second world conflict proposed that indemnity payments be exacted from the aggressors not in cash but in kind, thus avoiding the transfer difficulties that had been such a plague in the twenties. Payments were to be made largely from existing wealth (equipment, machine tools, ships, rolling stock, completely equipped industrial enterprises, and so on), with annual deliveries from current production extending over a limited number of years.

The purpose of this section is to present a brief historical survey, beginning with the Franco-Prussian indemnity of 1871 and extending through the close of World War II, from which it can be concluded that the form of reparations imposed upon the aggressors in the middle 1940s represented an endeavor to avoid the international trade problems and to treat such unilateral payments as being essentially domestic in nature.

Franco-Prussian Indemnity

The Franco-Prussian indemnity of 1871 introduced into international trade theory a series of complex problems by creating a precedent for German reparations after World War I when the conditions basic to the payments were altogether different. Germany, after winning the brief war of 1870, levied upon the French an indemnity of approximately 5 billion francs, which was to be transferred in several large installments. Little more than 500 million francs were paid in gold and silver coin, and in German coin spent in France by German troops, which left nearly 4.5 billion to be paid in foreign exchange.

France raised the franc value of the indemnity by two large loans, which amounted to 5.8 billion francs. A considerable part of the subscription of these loans came from abroad, both from foreigners who found the investment attractive and from Frenchmen who sold foreign investments. Both forms of subscriptions created foreign exchange which the French government purchased with the proceeds of the loan in effecting payments.

The real transfer was subsequently brought about by relative deflation in France as a result of increased taxes and higher rates of interest and by general inflation in Germany—a result of the acquisition of additional gold in part payment of the indemnity and the shift of the German monetary standard from bimetallism, in which both gold and silver were included in reserves, to gold alone. Depreciating the franc relative to the mark had the effect of creating a French export surplus and a German import surplus thus transferring capital in the real sense from the debtor to the creditor.

The difficulty posed for trade theory by the Franco-Prussian indemnity was that it made reparation payments appear transferable between countries, with little concern about the basic underlying conditions. In retrospect, one might conclude, however, that it was possible to effect such a unilateral transfer only because France was willing to deflate and because Germany acquiesced by permitting an increase in spending. In contrast, the failure to transfer German reparations after World War I made clear that the experience of 1871 had been a special, not a general, case.[1]

That reparations would be required from a defeated Germany in 1919 followed automatically from the facts of 1871. But in order for such payments to be effected it was necessary either to duplicate the position of 1871 or to create an equivalent set of circumstances. Unfortunately, neither condition was met.

---

[1]For a discussion of the Franco-Prussian indemnity see Charles P. Kindleberger, *International Economics* (rev. ed.; Homewood, Ill.: Richard D. Irwin, Inc., 1958), pp. 361–63.

German Reparations after World War I

The reparation clauses of the Treaty of Versailles established German obligation to the following liability:

> The Allied and Associated Governments affirm and Germany accepts the responsibility of Germany and her allies for causing all the loss and damage to which the Allied and Associated Governments and their nationals have been subjected as a consequence of the war imposed upon them by the aggression of Germany and her allies.[2]

Furthermore,

> The Allied and Associated Governments . . . require, and Germany undertakes, that she will make compensation for all damage done to the civilian population of the Allied and Associated Powers and to their property during the period of the belligerency of each as an Allied or Associated Power against Germany by such aggression by land, by sea and from the air, and in general all damage as defined in Annexe I hereto.[3]

The history of the German indemnity payments divides itself into three distinct chapters: From 1920 to 1924, the execution of the treaty was in the hands of the Reparation Commission; from 1924 to 1930 reparations were governed by the Dawes Plan; from 1930 to 1931, they were governed by the Young Plan; and in 1932 they were suspended and finally cancelled.

The Reparation Commission

Germany's total liability was to be determined by a reparation commission composed of representatives of the Allied and Associated Powers. The commission was to fix the amount of the installments for a period of 30 years, any unpaid balance at the end of this period being "postponed" or "handled other-

---

[2]Philip Mason Burnett. *Reparations at the Paris Peace Conference from the Standpoint of the American Delegation,* Vol. II, Doc. 440 (New York: Columbia University Press, 1940), p. 215.

[3]*Ibid.*, p. 216.

wise," and to supervise the management of the debt, its collection and its distribution among the Allied and Associated creditors.

In short, the treaty, while establishing German liability, did not define the total sum to be paid as reparations, but rather specified a minimum debt of 100 billion gold marks. It left to the Reparation Commission the task of fixing the total debt not later than May 1, 1921, and of administering its payments over a 30-year period.

Although the final amount of the liability was not determined, various tentative estimates were nevertheless set forth as indicating the magnitude of the anticipated bill or anticipated claims for damage which were to be submitted to the Reparation Commission by the Allied governments. These estimates for the most part, according to John Maynard Keynes, were grossly exaggerated and represented a hopeless miscalculation of Germany's capacity to pay.[4]

On May 1, 1921, the Reparation Commission set the total liability for damage to be made good by Germany under reparations at 132 billion marks. At the same it asserted, in the face of German protests, that less than half the payments Germany had agreed to make prior to May 1 had actually been received. Subsequently the Allies issued the so-called London Ultimatum which included the threat of Allied occupation of the Ruhr. Accordingly, Germany was to pay, in addition to the delivery of certain bonds, 2 billion marks annually plus a sum equivalent to 26 percent of the value of her exports.

"The probable burden of the new settlement in the near future," wrote Mr. Keynes, "is probably not much more than half that of the treaty."[5] And although it provided a transition from "foolish expectations," it could not be more than ". . . a temporizing measure which was bound to need amend-

[4]John Maynard Keynes, *The Economic Consequences of the Peace* (New York: Harcourt, Brace and Company, 1920), pp. 113–34.

[5]John Maynard Keynes, *A Revision of the Treaty* (New York: Harcourt, Brace and Company, 1922), p. 71.

ment."[6] "Sometime between February and August 1922 Germany will succumb to an inevitable default."[7]

We shall not be concerned with a detailed account of the transactions that followed between the imploring Reparation Commission and the dodging German government, but rather with a summary of the main events only. With the aid of short-term foreign credits, the first billion prescribed by the schedule was duly paid in August, 1921. However, by July, 1922, the German government, already in default, requested a two-year moratorium with a view to stabilizing the mark. Subsequently French and Belgian troops occupied the Ruhr district and all reparation deliveries ceased.

It is generally alleged that the occupation of the Ruhr, as the culmination of a period of reckless efforts to enforce the Treaty of Versailles, precipitated the final annihilation of the mark and the "collapse" of the German economy. The mark had depreciated continuously until in July, 1922, the rate was about 500 to the dollar. By November, 1923, a period when the German government was financing "passive resistance" by a massive issue of notes, the mark reached the incredible figure of 4.2 trillion to the dollar. The currency was then stabilized at the rate of 1 trillion paper marks for 1 renten mark.[8]

Dawes Plan

Upon request, the Reparation Commission in November, 1923, created the so-called Dawes Committee of experts to "consider the means of balancing the budget and the measures

---

[6]*Ibid.*, p. 73.

[7]*Ibid.*, p. 77.

[8]The above discussion of the German reparations between 1920 and 1924 was drawn from the following sources: Etienne Mantoux, *The Carthaginian Peace* (London: Oxford University Press, 1946), pp. 133–44; James W. Angell, *The Recovery of Germany* (New Haven: Yale University Press, 1929), pp. 17–60; Henri Lichtenberger, *Relations Between France and Germany* (Carnegie Endowment for International Peace and Education, No. 18) (Washington, D. C., 1923), pp. 100–124; and Costantino Bresciani-Turroni, *The Economics of Inflation* (London: George Allen and Unwin, Ltd., 1937).

to be taken to stabilize the currency;"[9] that is, to devise ways and means of procuring from Germany reparation payments consistent with a stabilized currency and a balanced budget—balanced in the sense that a surplus was to be available for reparation purposes. In their proposals no attempt was made to establish either the total sum to be paid as reparations or the duration of payments, but rather to establish a workable schedule of annuities; for the first two years, the annuities were to be 1,000 and 1,220 million marks, respectively, and by the fifth year there was to be a standard payment of 2,500 million marks.[10] A system of internal taxes and other levies to provide funds for the scheduled payments was set up. This, in effect, relieved the German government of current responsibility for meeting the charges as long as the "Dawes Plan revenue" was adequate. If, however, the yield became insufficient, the whole budget of the government was liable. In the last analysis reparations were a "first charge" on the total assets of Germany as long as the original provisions of the treaty remained in force.

Perhaps the most original feature of the plan was the solution given to the transfer problem. "There is," said the committee, "an important difference between Germany's capacity to pay taxes and Germany's capacity to transfer wealth abroad."[11] Accordingly, a transfer committee was to obviate the dangers to currency stability arising from excessive remittances; the annuities were to be paid in marks (as opposed to the currencies of the creditor powers) by the German government to the Agent General's account at the Reichsbank, and the committee was to decide how much could be transferred without endangering the currency.

During the following five years the annuities were paid regularly and transferred to the creditors without serious difficulty. But then a new factor had come into play: Germany's massive and continuous foreign borrowings.

---

[9]Angell, *op. cit.*, p. 62.
[10]Mantoux, *op. cit.*, p. 145.
[11]*Ibid.*

As soon as the mark had been stabilized in 1924 foreign capital began to pour into Germany. Between 1924 and 1930, the importation of long-term capital amounted to more than 9 billion marks, and the short-term credits to some 12 billion. To these sums must be added direct investment in real property, German securities, and so forth. This does not, however, represent the net inflow of capital, as a certain amount was also exported from Germany. It was calculated in August, 1931, that the net influx between 1924 and 1930 amounted to some 18 billion marks.[12] This corresponds closely to the estimated total debits of the German balance of payments during that period; and it explains why this balance, at a time when Germany was paying reparations, was constantly passive. In other words, the net importation of foreign capital by Germany during the period of the Dawes Plan was more than twice the amount of her reparation payments.

It was for this reason that the transfer safeguards provided by the Dawes Plan were never put into operation; there was always an excess of foreign exchange at the disposal of the German government and the stability of the mark was never endangered. But, at the same time, the importation of foreign capital had the effect of postponing the ultimate problem of German payments. That is, reparations were being paid, literally, with foreign loans and investments and not with the savings and taxes of the German people.

That the real problem of payment was thus being postponed was further emphasized by Mr. Keynes when he wrote, concerning the interdependence of war debts and reparations, "Reparations and Inter-Allied Debts are being mainly settled in paper and not in goods. The United States lends money to Germany, Germany transfers its equivalent to the allies, the allies pay it back to the United States Government. Nothing real passes—no one is a penny the worse."[13] The real question, however, was what was to happen when the foreign loans

[12]*Ibid.*, pp. 144–46.
[13]Mantoux, *op. cit.*, p. 148.

ceased. The German payments under the Dawes Plan were not in themselves proof that the system was workable.[14]

The Young Plan and the End of Reparations

The Dawes Plan had been conceived as a provisional settlement. It had left untouched the question of Germany's total liability, which remained in principle that fixed by the schedule of 1921, a total which the Dawes annuities would not have been sufficient to discharge. In 1929 the creditors assembled again, and after a series of negotiations adopted the proposals of a new committee of experts—the Young Plan.

The Young Plan was to be the final solution to the reparation problem. Germany's obligations were considerably reduced, and although the plan did not expressly fix the total value of the debt, it provided for 59 annual payments which totaled 121 billion marks; the present value of the annuities was estimated at 37 billion marks. Another feature of the plan was that the system of transfer protection was modified; Germany was again required to make payments in external currencies. Furthermore, all payments were to be made through the new Bank of International Settlements to which was assigned the administration of Germany's debt in the future.[15]

The new plan had scarcely begun to function when the Great Depression seized the world, the effects of which were particularly severe in Germany. By the end of 1931 the index of industrial production had fallen from 100 to 66; that is, one-third of the industrial life in Germany had stopped. Unemployment rose to a figure of 5 million. Depression per se might have improved the German payments position if it had not been for the financial crisis precipitated by the Austrian Credit Anstalt failure in May, 1931. Not only was the capital

---

[14]The above discussion of the Dawes Plan was taken from Mantoux, *op. cit.*, pp. 144–48; Harold G. Moulton (ed.), *The Reparation Plan* (New York: McGraw-Hill Book Company, 1924); Angell, *op. cit.*, pp. 61–80.

[15]Mantoux, *op. cit.*, p. 149.

flow into Germany halted but withdrawals of foreign credits took on alarming proportions. By June, the Reichsbank was facing withdrawals at the rate of 200 million marks per week, and the stock exchange was deteriorating rapidly. On June 29 President Hoover issued his proposal for a one-year moratorium on all reparations and inter-Allied debts. After somewhat difficult negotiations the moratorium was accepted and reparation payments were suspended—never to be resumed. Thus, once Germany ceased to receive foreign loans, the crisis became inevitable.

The negotiations of 1932 which led to the Lausanne agreements resulted in a final settlement and reparations were cancelled. Germany agreed to deliver to the Bank of International Settlements bonds totaling 3 billion marks, not to be issued before 3 years, any amount remaining unsold to be cancelled after 15 years. Thus did the reparations come to an end.

Economics of the Reparations

The depreciation of the German mark has often been ascribed to the adverse effect of reparation payments upon Germany's exchanges. It cannot be denied that the remittance of large sums abroad would have affected the exchange rate—depreciated the German Mark—yet it can hardly be maintained that the payment of less than 2 billion marks, which was the sum of cash indemnities between 1919 and the end of 1923, could have had the effect of annihilating the mark.

Doubtless the burdens imposed on Germany by the Treaty of Versailles contributed to the deficit shown in the years 1920–23. However, reparation charges explain less than a third of the total difference between expenditures and income which existed for 1920–23; that is, while the deficit amounted to some 10 billion gold marks before the signing of the treaty, between 1920 and 1923 it amounted to 18.7 billion.[16]

The depreciation of the mark was essentially due to infla-

---

[16]Bresciani-Turroni, *op. cit.*, pp. 93–94.

tion, a malady from which all countries in Europe suffered as a consequence of the war; while the German mark was reduced by more than 99.9 percent, the value of the French franc fell by more than 80 percent. After 1933, in preparation for rearmament, Germany, through a rigorous policy of taxation and exchange control, was able to finance public expenditures in excess of those demanded by reparation without the adverse effects of a seriously depreciating currency. Stabilization after 1919 might have been possible through similar measures if the German government had been ready to put a stop to the issue of notes.

It is interesting to consider the real burden supported by Germany during the reparations. We have already seen that after 1924 foreign borrowing permitted Germany to postpone the ultimate problem of payments, in that reparations were being paid with money from foreign sources rather than from the savings and taxes of the German people. Furthermore, it is pointed out that before 1923 a large quantity of German bank notes and balances were purchased by foreigners at a time when the German exchange was rapidly deteriorating in anticipation that the mark would eventually recover to par. It was estimated that by 1924 such sales amounted to from 7.6 to 8.7 billion marks. "What Germany has appeared to pay in reparations," observed Mr. Keynes, "is nearly equal to what the foreign world has subscribed in return for worthless marks."[17] Such was Germany's burden after the Treaty of Versailles.

Few questions have provided more food for debate, political and academic, than the transfer aspects of the German reparations problem. The actual detail of both the monetary and the real transfer mechanism precipitated an intensified controversy which assisted in developing certain aspects of international trade theory.

That Germany could only pay by an increase in exports was never open to discussion. (A country receives capital from

---

[17]Mantoux, *op. cit.*, p. 154.

abroad in a real sense only when it receives goods or services over and above the value of the goods it exports, and lends or pays abroad when it produces more than it consumes or invests at home, the difference representing the excess of exports over imports.) Even if Germany had been able to pay her creditors in marks, what the creditors ultimately wanted were real goods. Writes Mr. Keynes:

> It is certain that an annual payment can only be made by Germany over a series of years by diminishing her imports and increasing her exports, thus enlarging the balance in her favor which is available for effecting payments abroad. Germany can pay in the long-run in goods, and in goods only, whether these goods are furnished direct to the Allies, or whether they are sold to neutrals and the neutral credits so arising are then made over to the Allies.[18]

This principle is also reflected in the report of the Second Subcommittee at the Peace Conference. Noting that before the war, Germany's merchandise exports were generally less than her imports, they concluded that

> . . . in order to reverse this trade balance so that Germany's annual exports may largely exceed its imports, the industrial and domestic life of Germany must adapt itself and cut down imports to the least figure commensurate with the amount of raw materials which she actually requires from abroad for the conduct of her domestic and industrial life; and must turn herself into a nation of exporters, organized for the purpose of paying the reparation claims.[19]

In 1929, Keynes, in an article which stressed the difficulties Germany would encounter even if she succeeded in providing for the payments in the government budget, suggested that in order to adjust the German trade balance to its reparation obligations—increased exports relative to imports—not only must the price of German exports fall but exports must be of such a nature that sales would increase proportionately more than the fall in price. That is, if the elasticity of demand for German exports were less than unity, a given price reduction would result in a less than proportionate increase in demand and as such it would be impossible to expand export receipts

---

[18]Keynes, *Economic Consequences*, *op. cit.*, p. 188.
[19]Burnett, *op. cit.*, Doc. 543, p. 752.

by lowering prices. Thus he concluded that reparations in this case could not be transferred even if relative price changes did occur, or for such transfer to occur "... the expenditure of the German people must be reduced, not only by the amount of the reparation taxes which they must pay out of their earnings, but also by a reduction in their gold-rate of earnings below what they would otherwise be,"[20] that is, wages and so forth would fall more than if taxes were extracted alone.

Ohlin, the principal critic of the Keynsian thesis, on the other hand, discounted the effects of price elasticities and focused attention on the possibility that the transfer would be effected not through price shifts but through changes in income.[21] He failed, however, to perceive that none of the countries involved was pursuing the internal policies which such a transfer called for.

It is sufficient to observe here, however, that for the period considered Germany did not achieve a surplus of exports over imports. Furthermore, the balance of payments indicates that until 1931 capital imports into Germany were consistently in excess of capital exports.

One final point to be mentioned, one from which much criticism has derived, is the avoidance of establishing a definite sum representing Germany's liability. It would appear to have been advantageous to both the debtor and the creditors to have known, on the one hand, what was required by way of payment and on the other, what was to be received. Of this Keynes writes:

> There are no precedents for the indemnity imposed on Germany under the present treaty; for the money extractions which formed part of the settlement after previous wars have differed in two fundamental respects from this one. The sum demanded has been determinate and has been measured in a lump sum of money; and as long as the defeated party was meeting the annual installments of cash no consequential interference was necessary.[22]

[20] John Maynard Keynes, "The German Transfer Problem," *Economic Journal,* Vol. XXXIX, March, 1929, p. 4.

[21] Bertil Ohlin, "The Reparation Problem: A Discussion," *Economic Journal,* Vol. XXXIX, June, 1929, pp. 172–73.

[22] Keynes, *Economic Consequences, op. cit.,* p. 208.

This brief survey will serve to indicate that, unlike the earlier Franco-Prussian indemnity, the debtor did not deflate, nor did the creditors expand expenditures to produce, respectively, an export and an import surplus. To the extent that the German government raised the reparation payments through taxation (principally after the currency stabilization) its policy was deflationary in nature. However:

> . . . the increase in the rate of interest and the enthusiasm of the international investment bankers in New York defeated this. Governmental deflation at the national level was offset by provincial and local inflation, as industry and local governments borrowed abroad for spending on balance.[23]

Nor did Britain and France adjust their spending to fit projected reparation receipts. Such receipts were regarded not as a new source of income to be spent, thus raising national income, but as a means of debt reduction. Reparations failed both to contract expenditure in the paying country and to enlarge expenditures in the receiving countries. Transfer proved impossible except on the basis of borrowed funds.

Reparations After World War II

That Germany and the Axis Powers should be made incapable of renewing their enterprise of conquest at the end of the second world conflict, and that they be compelled to make the largest possible contribution to the recovery of the countries, which, directly or indirectly, bore the consequence of their actions was demanded by the interest of all. Recognizing, however, the extreme difficulties experienced in the twenties—the problems of the German reparation payments owed to the Allies, the war debts owed to the United States, and the closely related large-scale outflow of American capital —the impositions of the current indemnities followed a form which was essentially designed to eliminate the so-called transfer problem.

---

[23]Kindleberger, *op. cit.*, 1958, p. 362.

At the various peace conferences—Cairo, Teheran, Yalta, Potsdam and others—the governments of the United States, the Union of Soviet Socialist Republics, and the United Kingdom agreed upon the principles to be followed in the exaction of indemnity payments from the defeated powers. The World War I concept of reparations as the maximum obtainable financial compensation—undefined sums of money for the staggering costs of war—was abandoned. In order to avoid, among other problems, the transfer of indemnity burden from debtor to creditors, through the repudiation of loans and so forth, as was the case in the twenties, the following two principles were agreed upon: The primary objective was the establishment of both military and economic security against renewed aggression, not the maximization of reparation payments, and the reparations should be paid in kind rather than in cash, the payment in kind to be made from such assets as would, if left under their (the Axis Powers) control, constitute an economic base for future aggression, but would, if received as reparations, hasten economic recovery of the Allied Powers.

At the Yalta Conference the Soviet proposal for exacting reparations from Germany was set forth as follows:

> Our plan forsees that reparations in kind should be demanded from Germany in two ways. First, withdrawals from the national wealth of Germany. That means factories, land, machinery, machine tools, rolling stock of railroads, investments in foreign enterprises, and so on. Second, yearly payments in kind after the war in the course of ten years.[24]

It was further emphasized that reparations should be a fixed amount—$20 billion in the case of Germany.

Mr. Churchill, recalling the experience of the United Kingdom after World War I remarked:

> The process was a very disappointing one. With great difficulty about 1,000 million pounds was extracted from Germany, and that would never have been extracted if the United States, at the same time, had not loaned Germany a larger sum.[25]

---

[24]James F. Byrnes, *Speaking Frankly* (New York: Harper and Brothers, 1947), p. 26.

[25]*Ibid.*, p. 27.

He then declared that the "Removal of plants and factories to a certain extent is a proper step." To this Marshal Stalin added: "The root of the trouble the last time, was that reparations were demanded in money. Then, the question arose of transferring the German mark into foreign currencies. That was the rock upon which reparations broke down."[26]

The Allied Commission on Reparations set forth the following basic principles regarding indemnity payments: (1) Removals of property for reparations shall be primarily such as to assist in bringing to an end the war-making power of the aggressors by eliminating that part of their industrial capacity which constitutes war potential; (2) any plan of reparations shall be avoided which necessitates external financial assistance either to enable reparation deliveries to be made or to facilitate economic reconstruction required for reparation purposes; (3) to a maximum extent reparations shall be taken from existing national wealth. For convenience, claims may be stated in money. However it is necessary to bear in mind that in contrast to reparations after World War I, which were both assessed and exacted in money, currently reparations will be assessed and exacted in kind, plants, machines, equipment, stocks, and so on.[27]

Even though we are not expressly concerned with German reparations after World War II, the above defines and sets forth the basic principles underlying reparations in general, and, in particular, the reparations imposed upon Finland by the U.S.S.R. in the armistice concluded on September 19, 1944.

As early as 1943, when the Allied Powers were convened at the Teheran Conference, the question of Finland's independence and her obligation to pay compensation for war damages became a point of issue. The Soviets indicated that ". . . Russia had no designs on the independence of Finland, if Finland

---

[26] *Ibid.*, p. 28.

[27] U.S. Department of State, *Foreign Relations of the United States, Diplomatic Papers, The Conference of Berlin (The Potsdam Conference)*, 1960, Vol. II, Doc. 894, p. 833.

by its behavior did not force Russia to do so."[28] Marshal Stalin emphasized, however, that even though it had been said that an indemnity could not be extracted from a country such as Finland, ". . . payments in kind over a period of from 5 to 8 years, such as timber, paper and other materials would cover some of the damage done by Finland during the war, and that the Soviet Government intended to demand such reparation."[29] Subsequently, the Soviets expressed a willingness to open peace negotiations with the Finns provided that such negotiations be based on the following conditions:

(1) The restoration of the treaty of March, 1940, and the re-establishment of the frontiers set forth in that treaty.

(2) The Finnish Army to be demobilized to peacetime strength.

(3) Finland to pay reparations in kind for 50 percent of the physical damage done to the Soviet Union because of Finnish participation in the war against the Soviet Union. These reparations in kind to be paid over a period of from five to eight years and if Finland should default the Red Army will occupy certain areas of Finland.

(4) Finland to break off all association with Germany and expel the German forces from her territory.[30]

On September 19, 1944, the Finno-Russian armistice was signed obligating Finland not only to pay an indemnity in kind (timber products, paper, cellulose, seagoing and river craft, sundry machinery, and so on) but to comply with the remaining above-mentioned terms of the negotiations.

Implications of Finnish Reparations

Thus we see that reparations following World War II were designed to minimize the problems of international trade which had been encountered in the twenties and to work these

[28]U.S. Department of State, *Foreign Relations of the United States, Diplomatic Papers, The Conferences at Cairo and Teheran,* 1961, Proceedings of the Conference, p. 590.

[29]*Ibid.,* p. 591.

[30]*Ibid.,* Post-Conference Papers, p. 848.

reparations out, insofar as possible, on a domestic basis. The fact that payments were effected in kind eliminated both the exchange of internal for external currencies and the accompanying "real transfer" to be effected through an export surplus on the part of the debtor and a corresponding import surplus on the part of the creditor. Furthermore, the problem of Allied war debts was nonexistent in the sense that "Lend-Lease" was recognized as outright grants. There were, nevertheless, loans granted to certain of the defeated powers and, in addition, some countries had accumulated substantial external debts which may have given rise to problems not entirely dissimilar.

Finland, for example, was borrowing from both the United States and Great Britain, as well as from other foreign sources, at a time when she was making payments to the Soviet Union. The following set of data indicates the total amounts drawn and the total repaid between 1945 and 1952.

TABLE 2–1

FINNISH ANNUAL DRAWINGS AND REMITTANCES

1945–52

Year	Millions of marks		Equivalent in millions of dollars	
	Drawn	Repaid	Drawn	Repaid
1945	1,172	−99	27	−1
1946	10,771	−1,639	79	−12
1947	8,207	−6,476	60	−48
1948	7,221	−3,628	53	−27
1949	5,496	−4,969	30	−30
1950	3,571	−3,990	15	−17
1951	3,836	−10,123	17	−44
1952	3,015*	−5,054	13*	−22
Total	43,289	−35,978	294	−201

*In addition, $4.5 million was purchased from the IMF.

SOURCE: Bank of Finland, *Monthly Bulletin*, 1953, Vol. XXVII, Nos. 9–10.

Between 1945 and 1949 the amounts borrowed annually exceed the amounts redeemed. Subsequently, however, the amounts borrowed were less than redemptions. At the end of

1952 Finland's foreign long-term debt amounted to 64,487 million marks or nearly $280 million. At the previous peak of foreign borrowing, 1930, the long-term debt amounted to $206 million, based on the 1930 rate of exchange. If this amount is converted to 1952 dollars, adjusted for the depreciated value of the dollar between 1930 and 1952, it represents some $425 million.

Even though Finland was borrowing abroad at a time when she was paying reparations to the Soviet Union, the real burden of such payments cannot be considered as having been transferred to the creditor nations, as was the case in the twenties, when the incident of the burden was shifted from the debtor through the repudiation of loans and so forth (Table 2-2).

TABLE 2–2

FINLAND'S ANNUAL NET DRAWINGS AND REPARATION PAYMENTS 1945–52

(Millions of Marks)

Year	Net Drawings*	Reparations†
1945	1,073.0	8,171.5
1946	9,132.0	8,775.1
1947	1,731.0	10,404.7
1948	3,593.0	11,545.6
1949	527.0	12,226.3
1950	–419.0	7,845.8
1951	–6,287.0	12,396.4
1952	–2,039.0	8,215.4

*Source: Table 2–1, p. 38.
†Source: Table 1–1, p. 18.

Many of the loans granted Finland in the early indemnity years, such as credits received from the Export-Import Bank, were granted for the express purpose of acquiring machinery, appliances, and the necessary requisites for the construction and renovation of the woodworking industries, and for the rebuilding and expansion of power stations. To the extent that foreign capital was employed in building the industrial structure necessary to effect the indemnity payments, the burden of reparations was to some degree shared by foreign creditors. However, by 1950 redemption payments were in excess of new drawings, and, as such, it cannot logically be concluded that, even though Finland's creditors shared part of the indemnity burden in the initial years, the Finns paid their war obligation solely with foreign capital as was the case for what small remittances Germany made in the twenties.

For Finland, an indemnity such as was imposed might well be viewed as a contributing factor to the successful fulfillment of her war obligation while maintaining her identity as an independent state. From the outset of the peace negotiations, the Soviet government had emphasized that failure to meet the specified schedule of deliveries meant Russian military occupation of certain areas of Finland. The fact, however, that not only was a total liability established but that payments were to be made according to an exacting schedule permitted the Finns, by meeting the payments per schedule, to meter their own progress in discharging the responsibility and to demonstrate to the Soviet Union their sincerity in striving to make good damages caused by them in the war. This latter point, while not explicitly referred to in the negotiations, undoubtedly influenced to some extent the Soviet government to grant certain alleviations from the original schedule of deliveries and to refrain from invoking their threatened military occupation. On this point Keynes, in describing indemnities prior to 1919, wrote: "The sum demanded has been determinate and has been measured in a lump sum . . . and so long as the defeated party was meeting the annual installments . . . no consequential interference was necessary."[31] As a result of Finland's effecting annual installments according to the prescribed schedule, "no consequential interference was necessary."

In retrospect, however, it appears that this unilateral transfer to the Soviet Union, representing compensation for

[31]Keynes, *Economic Consequences*, *op. cit.*, p. 208.

war damage, was effected not as a result of the timetable of payments or the foreign capital or other influencing factors but rather because the Finns were desperately anxious to do so. This perhaps represents a direct contrast to the German situation after World War I.

With this brief survey of the Finnish indemnity of 1944 and of reparations in general we turn our attention to the development and application of an input-output technique in an empirical investigation of the interindustrial relationships that existed within the Finnish economy during the period of indemnity payments—that is, to determine the impact of the reparations on the various interdependent industries comprising the economy and to arrive at a real cost involved in effecting the deliveries.

The following two sections will be concerned with a theoretical description of the particular technique used and the final two sections with the empirical implications.

3

BASIC MODEL

Open and Closed Static Input-Output Systems

Input-output analysis is essentially an attempted application of the theory of general equilibrium to empirical quantitative analysis of a given national economy. The economy is visualized as a combination of a large number of interdependent activities; that is, of various branches of production, distribution, transportation, consumption, and so on. Each one of these activities involves the purchase of commodities and services originating in other branches of the economy on the one hand, and the production of commodities and services which are sold to and absorbed by other sectors of the economy on the other. More specifically, an economy considered within the framework of an input-output system is regarded as made up of n sectors or industries for each of which a homogeneous additive measure of output or activity is assumed available. Each industry or sector requires certain inputs which it acquires from other sectors; it then sells its output to other sectors to meet their input requirements.

The "industry," defined as households, for example, furnishes its output (services) to other industries in return for consumer goods (household inputs). Government may be treated as an industry which makes payments to other sectors of the economy in return for goods or services and which provides services (its output), the costs of which are met principally by tax levies on the other sectors of the economy. Foreign trade may also be treated as an industry whose inputs are exports and whose product or output is imports. These commodity and service flows (transfers) taking place between the various sectors comprising the economy within some specified period of time, say a year, can be conveniently described by an input-output matrix. The allocation of the total output of any one industry among all the others is shown by a sequence of entries along a particular row, while the distribution of all inputs absorbed by any one industry by origin is at the same time represented by a sequence of entries in the appropriate input column.

Having given this description of the system of interindustrial relationships, we turn to the theoretical problem of its explanation. The input-output method depends upon two fundamental kinds of relationships: First, the identity that total output of any given industry is absorbed either by itself or by other industries. This identity can be conveniently represented by a set of balance equations. Second, the technological relationship that purchases of any sector from any other sector depend, via a production function, on the level of output of the purchasing sector. Equations (1) represent in generalized form the former of the two relationships—the distribution of each industry's output.

$$\begin{array}{l} (X_1 - x_{11}) - x_{12} - \dots - x_{1i} - \dots - x_{1n} = 0 \\ -x_{21} + (X_2 - x_{22}) - \dots - x_{2i} - \dots - x_{2n} = 0 \\ \dots\dots\dots\dots\dots\dots\dots\dots\dots \\ -x_{i1} - x_{i2} - \dots + (X_i - x_{ii}) - \dots - x_{in} = 0 \\ \dots\dots\dots\dots\dots\dots\dots\dots\dots \\ -x_{n1} - x_{n2} - \dots - x_{ni} - \dots + (X_n - x_{nn}) = 0 \end{array} \qquad (1)$$

where $X_i \geq 0$ denotes the total physical output of the ith industry in units of a dollar's worth of its product in some base year, and $x_{ij} \geq 0$ denotes the amount of product of the ith industry absorbed by the jth industry. It is assumed that all entries are nonnegative and that some (to insure nontriviality) are positive numbers.

The second or technological relationship may be expressed as follows: Ruling out joint production and assuming constant returns to scale, we may write the production function relating the output X_j to its inputs x_{ij} as

$$X_j = f(x_{1j}, x_{2j}, \ldots, x_{nj}), \quad (j = 1, 2, \ldots, n) \tag{2}$$

where f is a homogeneous function of degree 1. We can also assume that the isoquant surfaces have the usual convexity;[1] that is to say, we can assume diminishing returns. The distinctive feature of input-output analysis is that it makes not only both of the above assumptions but the far stronger one of fixed coefficients of production; that is, that a certain minimum amount of each input is required per unit of each output.

If we let a_{ij} be the required minimum amount of the ith input per unit of the jth output, then (2) can be written as

$$X_j = \min\left[\frac{x_{1j}}{a_{1j}}, \frac{x_{2j}}{a_{2j}}, \ldots, \frac{x_{nj}}{a_{nj}}\right], \quad (j = 1, 2, \ldots, n) \tag{3}$$

Since X_j equals the smallest of x_{1j}/a_{1j}, x_{2j}/a_{2j}, . . ., x_{nj}/a_{nj} it follows that

$$X_j \leq x_{ij}/a_{ij}, \quad \begin{matrix}(j = 1, 2, \ldots, n)\\(i = 1, 2, \ldots, n)\end{matrix} \tag{4}$$

and since no more than the limitational amount of any input

[1]The assumption of fixed coefficients implies a production function of the form

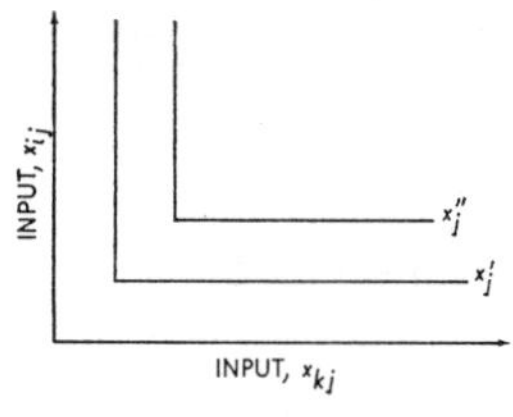

as opposed to the more general form admitting substitution between inputs. In the case of fixed coefficients, excesses of any one input contribute nothing to production, while shortages of any one input limit the output that can be produced.

will be used the equality sign will hold and (4) can be written as

$$x_{ij} = a_{ij}X_j, \qquad \begin{matrix} (j = 1, 2, \ldots, n) \\ (i = 1, 2, \ldots, n) \end{matrix} \tag{5}$$

These considerations reveal the basic assumption of the method, namely, that the quantity of each input consumed by a sector is directly proportional to the quantity of output produced by it. The factors of proportionality, the a_{ij}s, show the requirements of the *i*th input needed to produce a single unit of the *j*th output. Thus the input-output structure of any one industry can be described by a set of "technical coefficients" each of which states the amount of each particular input absorbed by that industry per unit of its own output. (Since an industry may use some of its own output, there may be nonzero diagonal coefficients a_{11}, a_{22}, . . ., a_{nn}. Thus output X_i need not equal sales to other industries.)

Under the assumptions listed the economic system may be represented by the following set of linear homogeneous equations.

$$\begin{array}{l} (X_1 - a_{11}X_1) - a_{12}X_2 - \ldots - a_{1i}X_i - \ldots - a_{1n}X_n = 0 \\ -a_{21}X_1 + (X_2 - a_{22}X_2) - \ldots - a_{2i}X_i - \ldots - a_{2n}X_n = 0 \\ \cdots\cdots\cdots\cdots\cdots\cdots\cdots\cdots \\ -a_{i1}X_1 - a_{i2}X_2 - \ldots + (X_i - a_{ii}X_i) - \ldots - a_{in}X_n = 0 \\ \cdots\cdots\cdots\cdots\cdots\cdots\cdots\cdots \\ -a_{n1}X_1 - a_{n2}X_2 - \ldots - a_{ni}X_i - \ldots + (X_n - a_{nn}X_n) = 0 \end{array} \tag{6}$$

Since the number of equations in (6) equals the number of unknowns a necessary and sufficient condition for a nontrivial solution is that the determinant of the coefficients vanish, that is, $|\mathbf{A}| = 0$.[2]

The above describes a so-called closed input-output system. The consumption of all sectors is explained within the model in the course of determining the levels of output of the house-

[2]G. Hadley, *Linear Algebra* (Reading, Mass.: Addison-Wesley Publishing Company, Inc., 1961), p. 174.

hold, government, and other sectors which form part of a mutually consistent pattern of sector output levels. However, the problem with which we are to concern ourselves is best considered within the framework of an open input-output system. In such a system the coefficients in (6) are treated, more or less, as technological data. However, some of the outputs are assumed to be determined "outside the model," leaving the others to be calculated. In such calculations, a known set of coefficients and a partial list of outputs is used to predict the remaining outputs.

A closed system becomes open as soon as one or more of the basic structural relationships of which it has been made up is disregarded. A system is thus said to be open with respect to consumer demand if it does not contain equations describing the structural characteristics of the household sector, or it may be considered open with respect to investment demand, which implies that the structural relationships determining investment requirements of all the individual sectors of the economy are not included in the system.

Thus reduced, the number of available equations becomes insufficient to determine uniquely the magnitude of all the unknown variables. However, if arbitrary magnitudes are prescribed to some of these values, the corresponding magnitudes of all the other variables can be determined on the basis of the still available equations. That is to say, ". . . in an open system it is possible to fix a certain number of variables by deliberate choice while the remaining will fall in line in accordance with the existing necessities of the still inviolate structural relationships."[3]

Consider a system of m (independent) equations in n variables, with n being larger than m. If the values of any $n - m$ of these n variables are fixed, it can be solved for the remaining m. For example, in equation system (6) choose the last sector as one whose final demand is to be fixed and eliminate

[3]Wassily Leontief, "Input-Output Analysis and Its Use in Peace and War Economics," *American Economic Review*, Vol. XXXIX, May, 1949, No. 3, Papers and Proceedings of the Sixty-First Annual Meeting, p. 214.

the last equation. The resulting nonhomogeneous set of equations is as follows:

$$-a_{i1}X_1 - a_{i2}X_2 - a_{i3}X_3 - \ldots + (1 - a_{ii})X_i - \ldots - a_{im}X_m = a_{in}X_n, \quad (i = 1, 2, \ldots, m) \tag{7}$$

where $m = (n - 1)$.

By virtue of (5) we substitute $x_{1n}, x_{2n}, \ldots, x_{mn}$ for $a_{1n}X_n$, $a_{2n}X_n, \ldots, a_{mn}X_n$, respectively.

$$-a_{i1}X_1 - a_{i2}X_2 - a_{i3}X_3 - \ldots + (1 - a_{ii})X_i - \ldots - a_{im}X_m = X_{in}, \quad (i = 1, 2, \ldots, n) \tag{8}$$

where the x_{in}s are considered as a fixed "bill of goods," in terms of which the system of equations can be solved.

The "bill of goods" shows the distribution of output of each of the m sectors to the nth, or the demand by the nth sector for the output of the rest of the economy. If the nth sector consists of household and foreign trade the bill of goods can be interpreted as the final demand by consumers for the output of domestic industry. There is clearly a wide choice regarding which sources of demand are to be included in the autonomous sector—final demand—and which are to be explained within the model. This choice depends particularly on the disposition to be made of government demand, household consumption, net exports, and investment.

To recapitulate briefly the hypotheses underlying the open, static Leontief model, consider an economy in which there are m commodities independent of the primary factors. Each commodity is produced in one and only one industry following a uniquely given production technique. Each industry produces only one commodity. The technical processes are defined by the inputs required to produce a unit of output: a_{ij} is the quantity of the ith commodity required in the production of one unit of commodity j. It is assumed that processing n units implies the use of n times as much of each input. Hence, there are constant returns to scale everywhere and no possibility of technical substitution between the various inputs.

Referring to equation (8), the elements $0 \leq a_{ij} \leq 1$ collectively form a square m order matrix A. For the matrix $(I - A)$, the conditions given are sufficient to guarantee that it is nonsingular.[4] Using Y to represent the bill of goods vector and X the activity level vector the above system may appear in the following matrix forms

$$\begin{bmatrix} (1 - a_{11}) - a_{12} - \ldots - a_{1i} - \ldots - a_{1m} \\ -a_{21} + (1 - a_{22}) - \ldots - a_{2i} - \ldots - a_{2m} \\ \ldots\ldots\ldots\ldots\ldots\ldots \\ -a_{i1} - a_{i2} - \ldots + (1 - a_{ii}) - \ldots - a_{im} \\ \ldots\ldots\ldots\ldots\ldots\ldots \\ -a_{m1} - a_{m2} - \ldots - a_{mi} - \ldots + (1 - a_{mm}) \end{bmatrix} \begin{bmatrix} X_1 \\ X_2 \\ \vdots \\ X_i \\ \vdots \\ X_m \end{bmatrix} = \begin{bmatrix} Y_1 \\ Y_2 \\ \vdots \\ Y_i \\ \vdots \\ Y_m \end{bmatrix} \qquad (9)$$

or

$$(I - A)X = Y \qquad (10)$$

Solving for the Xs we get

$$X = (I - A)^{-1}Y \qquad (11)$$

Thus given any desired outside bill of goods, $Y^\circ_1, Y^\circ_2, \ldots, Y^\circ_m$, and the technological structure embodied in the static functions, the corresponding set of production levels, $X_1, X_2, \ldots, X_m$, can be determined, if any such set exists.

The elements of $(I - A)^{-1}$ represent the total production requirements, direct and indirect, of each good needed for each unit of final demand and are in general functions of most or all of the parameters a_{ij}; A_{ij} is the total direct and indirect output of the ith commodity needed per unit of final consumption of the jth commodity and depends upon the input coefficients of all industries.

The conceptual framework of the system of interindustrial relationships outlined above, when applied to the postwar Finnish economy, permits us to determine, for each industry or sector contained within the system, a quantitative measure

[4] W. Duane Evans, "The Effects of Structural Matrix Errors on Interindustry Relations Estimates," *Econometrica*, Vol. 22, No. 4, October, 1954, p. 462.

of the reparations impact. That is, given the technological structure embodied in the a_{ij}s and two outside bills of goods, one of which contains payments to the Soviet Union under the reparations account, Y', and one from which such payments have been eliminated, Y'', production levels corresponding to each of the outside bills of goods can be determined by the equation system as follows:

$$X' = (I - A)^{-1}Y' \tag{12}$$

$$X'' = (I - A)^{-1}Y'' \tag{13}$$

where Y'_i differs from Y''_i by a factor equal to the indemnity payments from the ith sector. The difference between corresponding output levels, $X'_i - X''_i$ $(i = 1, 2, \ldots, m)$ *then* represents the impact of reparations on the individual industries or sectors comprising the economy.

Invariance of the Structural Coefficients

The matrix $(I - A)$, each column of which comprises the input coefficients of one particular industry, defines the technological structure of the particular system under consideration. Systems with identical sets of input coefficients are said to be structurally identical and systems with unlike input coefficients structurally different. Structural change, in other words, can be interpreted as a change in the technical matrix of the system.

According to the general conceptual framework thus outlined, an increase or decrease in the output, X_i, of any industry can be the result of a change in the given bill of goods, a change in the structure of the system, or a combination of both. Therefore the usefulness of the static input-output approach is conditioned by and depends upon the relative invariance of the structural characteristics. Indeed, Leontief accepts the a_{ij}s as having a considerable amount of invariance. With some oversimplification, the nature of this invariance may be stated as follows: Suppose that the a_{ij}s have been computed on the basis of a given year's data. Imagine now that the same year is to be "relived" by the nation, with a different bill of goods and a different set of outputs. Again, the a_{ij}s are computed from the "relived" year's data. They would be the same as those originally obtained; that is, the input-output coefficients are invariant to changes in both final demand and output levels. However, the postulate of invariance of the structural coefficients also implies that the a_{ij}s remain stable over time, as well. That is, the input-output coefficients at some time t are the same as those at some other time $t + 1$. This assumption is necessarily implicit in using the coefficients estimated from observations on one time period as part of a model for predicting the behavior of the economy in another time period. Thus not only is it necessary to assume constancy of the structural coefficients for purposes of estimation but over time as well, if any useful application of the results is to be made.

It is a key fact, however, that, while there may be many reasonably stable or predictable elements within the structural makeup, economic systems are, for the most part, constantly changing. No careful economic analysis can afford wholly to ignore the fact of change. Comparing the structure of an economic system in two stages of its development sufficiently removed from each other might well indicate that the input-output coefficients are not immutable, but rather are changing or varying with time.

The assumption that each industry has a production function in which all inputs vary proportionately with the industry's output—a linear function through the origin—is a marked variation from the more general S-shaped function exhibiting in various phases increasing, constant, and decreasing returns. If held strictly, this assumption implies that all inputs are uniformly affected by a change in the scale of production, ignoring the distinction between fixed and variable inputs and between short and long run; that industries can be classified sufficiently finely to eliminate multiproduct industries whose input structures would be affected by changes in the product mix of their outputs; that substitutions among inputs due to changes in the relative prices or availabilities are of negligible importance; and that technological changes in input structures are either predictable or sufficiently infrequent so that explicit adjustments can be made for them.

The assumption that there is a constant ratio over time between the volume of production (output) in any industry and the quantities of products (inputs) which it absorbs from each of the other industries, even though input-output analysis has not always made it clear, can only be considered as a first approximation to the more complex production functions of the real world. Nonproportional inputs, changes in product mix, input substitutions, and technological changes do in fact occur.

Empirical evidence of direct comparisons of individual input ratios at different points in time supports the theory that the structural relationships should not be considered as immutable or unchanging, but rather as varying with time. For example, in a study prepared by Leontief involving direct comparison of input ratios from the three United States interindustrial relations studies—1919, 1929, and 1939, consolidated to a least common denominator of 13 industries—there is very little evidence supporting the stability of the input ratios. Between 1919 and 1929 only about a fifth of the coefficients varied less than 20 percent, and between 1929 and 1939 only about a third. In the first decade about a sixth varied more than 50 percent and in the second decade about a quarter.[5] It should be recognized that, as a result of the gross level of aggregation and the inaccuracy of the tabulations—large undistributed outputs particularly in the 1939 table—this is only a rough test of the assumption of structural invariance. A similar study with Japanese input-output tables for 1951 and 1954, aggregated into 36 sectors, seem to lend more support to the invariance hypothesis. More than three-fourths of the coefficients varied less than 20 percent.[6]

---

[5]Hollis B. Chenery, and Paul G. Clark, *Interindustry Economics* (New York: John Wiley and Sons, Inc., 1959), p. 159.

[6]*Ibid.*, p. 160.

The shorter interval of time is doubtless a major factor in the greater apparent stability of the coefficients and it is also likely that the statistical quality of the Japanese tables is considerably better than that of the earlier United States tables. Nevertheless, there is currently little evidence that technological structure, as defined by a set of input-output coefficients, remains unchanged over short as well as long periods of time.

Granted then that the input-output ratios are not constant in the strict sense of the word, the question may be asked: How much do changes in the coefficients change the structure of outputs (or prices) ? And, if these changes seem to be, in some sense, large, can one make any hypothesis about how the input-output coefficients might have changed?

Considered from the point of view of a particular industry, a change in the input ratios may reflect an adjustment occasioned by a change in the supply conditions of the factors or the demand conditions in the finished product market. It may also reflect changes in the available technology. In the case of an innovation or of a new process, the change in the observable input ratios represents the result of a deliberate choice between the old and the—previously unknown—new input combinations. Whether caused by new price conditions or a widening of the technological horizon, an introduction of new input ratios implies increased efficiency since the old ratios are technically still possible. Thus one would expect that a given final bill of goods would require gradually decreasing amounts of output of intermediate goods. In some sense then, on the average, input-output coefficients should decrease over time. But there is no reason why every coefficient should decrease, or why any particular coefficient should decrease.

Structural data should, therefore, be subjected to careful study, aimed at finding out whether changes in actual outputs are due solely to changes in final demand. If not, then it is necessary to determine, if possible, what changes in input-output coefficients may have taken place. If the data were available, one might compute empirically the input-output coefficients at frequent intervals. But since the data are not always available it is difficult and expensive to compute such coefficients. As a result, in practice it is necessary to infer, on the basis of theoretical considerations and indirect evidence, what may have happened in some period for which actual coefficients are not available.

Input-Output Study for Postwar Finland

Payments made by Finland to the Soviet Union during the indemnity period constituted an important part of "final demand" for Finnish output. The effect of these payments is then, in principle, measurable. Compare two sets of final demands, one including and one excluding reparations; each set implies some (other) set of gross output. By comparing these outputs, some measure of the effect of reparation payments on each sector of the economy may be obtained. But, while it is easy to pose the problem as a simple one in input-output theory, its solution is not an easy one in detail. The difficulty arises because the relevant input-output matrices (the relevant sets of a_{ij}s) are not available. Only for 1956 is a matrix available, and we must attempt to determine what the matrix must have been like in the years during which reparation payments were actually taking place.

After a brief survey of input-output statistics available for the Finnish economy attention will be turned to the formulation of a theoretical framework. This framework will not only establish the existence or nonexistence of structural variation over time but will suggest—as a result of the basic underlying hypothesis which explains in part the pattern of change—a method of adjusting for certain of these changes.

Statistical investigation of interindustrial relations for the Finnish economy was first carried out by Osmo Forssell and Paavo Grönlund for the year 1956.[7] Empirical work in this

[7]Osmo Forssell and Paavo Grönlund, *Panos-Tuotos-Tutkimus Suomen Talouselamasta, Vuonna, 1956* (Helsinki: 1960).

field has been limited to this single 39-order input-output tabulation, and since it rests on a rather narrow statistical base —existing Industrial Statistics of Finland—its reliability in certain respects may be uncertain. The individual sectors have been defined according to the industrial classification used in the Official Statistics of Finland, which, with few minor exceptions, are based on the *International Standard Industrial Classification of All Economic Activities* published by the United Nations.

Although in the initial stages of preparation some 70 producing sectors with 15 primary inputs and 3 entries comprising the bill of final demand were employed, in the final analysis these were aggregated into 39 producing sectors and 5 primary inputs, with the bill of final demand remaining unchanged.

The compilation of the 1956 study placed rather severe strains on available quantitative knowledge. Not only did gaps in statistical information become apparent but the cross-analysis of data within a conceptually consistent framework indicated serious inconsistencies in the data available (residual or unallocated flows). Thus, within the autonomous sector is included a column (and its corresponding row) labeled "undistributed" which contains both current flows, the distribution and destination of which could not be ascertained, and inventory changes which, as a result of lacking relevant statistics, were impossible to eliminate.

The application of input-output analysis to the postwar economy of Finland in determining the impact of the indemnity payments on the various interdependent industries or sectors comprising the economy necessitates an investigation of the following query. Since it is virtually impossible to acquire sufficient statistical information to compile an input-output tabulation for years prior to 1956, and since the indemnity period extended only through 1952, the current study is limited to the use of the 1956 structure or matrix of technical coefficients. However, it is only reasonable to assume the structural matrix invariant over time if a number of conditions are satisfied. Therefore, our analysis must necessarily be concerned with the relative stability of the individual coefficients comprising the structural matrix between the year of application (1952) and the base year (1956).

It might be assumed on the one hand, that changes in input-output patterns for the period under study would not materially affect the results and the 1956 matrix of technical coefficients would thus be employed with the 1952 final bill of demand in analyzing the effects of the 1952 indemnity payments; that is, the simultaneous input-output equations would be solved with the 1952 final bill of goods but would be based on technology as it existed in 1956. On the other hand there is no assurance that if the data (technical coefficients) on which the production level estimates are based had been established for the year 1952 instead of for 1956 the results would agree identically. Even though it is reasonable to expect a given technical matrix to be useful in explaining economic phenomena over a period of a few years, the structural coefficients are nevertheless subject to technological as well as other changes which in principle cannot be ignored. If, therefore, the estimated 1952 outputs differ from those that actually occurred we must consider how the structural matrix of the system might have changed. Hence the application of 1956 coefficients to 1952 data represents a first approximation to an answer which it may be possible to improve upon.

4

STRUCTURAL STABILITY AND TRANSFORMATION

Determining the Relative Stability of the Structural Coefficients by Comparing Calculated with Observed Prices

The following discussion suggests a method of generating, within an open static input-output framework, price data corresponding to the individual sectors. Such data can then be compared with actual price data in determining the stability of the coefficients over time. A necessary but not sufficient condition for the invariance of the technical coefficients, a_{ij}s, over time is that prices calculated on the basis of a given set of structural parameters do not vary from observed prices which prevailed in some period other than the base period. If, on the other hand, the two sets of prices vary widely the technical coefficients cannot be considered as invariant but rather as changing with time.

Consider first a system in long-run competitive equilibrium in which profits have been eliminated and in which there is only one homogeneous primary factor. Even though the original Leontief theory assumes nonzero profits for each industry there is nothing inherent in the system which prevents the assumption that profits are zero. Further assume that labor, which is treated as homogeneous, represents the sole primary input into the present system.

Under perfectly competitive "statical" conditions, the equilibrium price for each producible good must be exactly equal to its unit cost of production. The latter consists of the costs per unit of each intermediate input, plus direct labor costs. Thus for the output of each of the m sectors the following market conditions exist:

$$\begin{aligned} P_j &= f_j P_f + a_{1j}P_1 + a_{2j}P_2 + \ldots + a_{ij}P_i + \ldots + a_{mj}P_m \\ &= f_j P_f + \sum_{i=1}^{m} a_{ij}P_i \qquad (j = 1, 2, \ldots, m) \end{aligned} \tag{14}$$

where f_j represents the amount of the primary factor, labor, absorbed by the jth industry per unit of its output and P_f the price of the primary factor.

Now it is obvious that the absolute level of prices plays no role in the model as it has been described. It is impossible to solve for determinate prices of all $m + 1$ variables. Instead, however, we may designate any one price as numeraire and solve for the remaining m prices in relation to it. In the Leontief system, it is natural to choose the wage rate as numeraire and solve for the price structure (relative to wages): $(P_1/P_f, \ldots, P_m/P_f)$. Thus equation (14) may be expressed as

$$\begin{aligned} P'_1 &= f_1 + a_{11}P'_1 + a_{21}P'_2 + \ldots + a_{i1}P'_i + \ldots + a_{m1}P'_m \\ P'_2 &= f_2 + a_{12}P'_1 + a_{22}P'_2 + \ldots + a_{i2}P'_i + \ldots + a_{m2}P'_m \\ &\ldots \ldots \ldots \ldots \ldots \ldots \\ P'_i &= f_i + a_{1i}P'_1 + a_{2i}P'_2 + \ldots + a_{ii}P'_i + \ldots + a_{mi}P'_m \\ &\ldots \ldots \ldots \ldots \ldots \ldots \\ P'_m &= f_m + a_{1m}P'_1 + a_{2m}P'_2 + \ldots + a_{im}P'_i + \ldots + a_{mm}P'_m \end{aligned} \tag{15}$$

where $P'_i = \dfrac{P_i}{P_f} \qquad (i = 1, 2, \ldots, m).$

Equations (15) resemble those of the original system (8). Both involve $(a_{11}, a_{12}, \ldots, a_{m1}, a_{m2}, \ldots, a_{mm})$, the square array of nonlabor input coefficients. But there is an important difference: The a_{ij}s appearing in a particular equation of (8) appear in different equations of (15); those appearing in a particular equation of (15) appear in different equations of (8). More precisely, (15) and (8) have matrices which are *transposed.* An element in row i and column j of (8) reappears in (15) but in a different position, namely column i and row j. The variables in (8) are outputs, while in (15) they are prices. There is, therefore, a "duality" relationship between quantities and prices in the Leontief system: transpose the as of the quantity problem to derive the price problem; similarly, transpose the as of the price problem to derive the quantity problem.

In matrix terms (15) may be written as

$$\begin{bmatrix} P'_1 \\ P'_2 \\ \vdots \\ P'_i \\ \vdots \\ P'_m \end{bmatrix} = \begin{bmatrix} f_1 \\ f_2 \\ \vdots \\ f_i \\ \vdots \\ f_m \end{bmatrix} + \begin{bmatrix} a_{11} & a_{21} & \dots & a_{i1} & \dots & a_{m1} \\ a_{12} & a_{22} & \dots & a_{i2} & \dots & a_{m2} \\ \cdot & \cdot & \cdot & \cdot & \cdot & \cdot \\ a_{1i} & a_{2i} & \dots & a_{ii} & \dots & a_{mi} \\ \cdot & \cdot & \cdot & \cdot & \cdot & \cdot \\ a_{1m} & a_{2m} & \dots & a_{im} & \dots & a_{mm} \end{bmatrix} \begin{bmatrix} P'_1 \\ P'_2 \\ \vdots \\ P'_i \\ \vdots \\ P'_m \end{bmatrix} \tag{16}$$

or

$$P' = F + A_T P' \tag{17}$$

which can be solved to determine the m unknown price ratios.

$$(I - A)_T P' = F \tag{18}$$

$$P' = (I - A)_T^{-1} F \tag{19}$$

The relative prices thus obtained, P_i/P_f $(i = 1, 2, \dots, m)$, are completely determined by the matrix of production coefficients and the direct labor coefficients, and, as such, are independent of any other factors, in particular of the given bill of goods. Indeed, the above conceptual framework is one in which the structure of prices is determined by technological relationships only.

The choice of labor as the only primary factor in determining the unknown price ratios leads directly to a labor theory of value,[1] which is evidenced by the fact that the coefficient denoting the total labor costs of say the jth commodity will exactly equal P_j/P_f, the competitively determined price ratio of that output relative to the wage rate. From (19) it follows that

$$P'_T = F_T(I - A)^{-1} \tag{20}$$

If the total labor input for all industries, F_o, is defined as

$$F_o = f_1X_1 + f_2X_2 + \ldots + f_mX_m \tag{21}$$

it further follows that

$$F_o = F_TX = F_T(I - A)^{-1}Y \tag{22}$$

since

$$X = (I - A)^{-1}Y$$

and

$$F_o = P'_TY$$

Hence: $\dfrac{\partial F_o}{\partial Y_j} = P'_j$ where $P'_j = P_j/P_f$ (23)

Thus, the total labor cost of the jth good exactly equals P_j/P_f, the price of the jth good relative to the wage rate.

The usefulness of a general theoretical framework, when applied to a given empirical problem, however, depends upon the extent to which its basic assumptions are likely to be valid, and since the above system is restricted to a single homogeneous primary factor, its usefulness can be considered as seriously impaired. In order to carry the analysis beyond the confines of these initial stages additional primary factors need to be introduced into the equation system. Suppose, as in the case of the Finnish input-output model, that the value added sector consists of (1) labor income, (2) capital revenue, (3) depreciation, (4) indirect taxes minus subsidies, and (5) imports. If capital revenue and depreciation can be grouped together and indirect taxes minus subsidies are dis-

[1]Nicholas Georgescu-Roegen, *Activity Analysis of Production and Allocation*, Chapter X, "Some Properties of the Generalized Leontief Model," (New York: John Wiley and Sons, Inc., 1951), p. 165.

regarded the analysis would involve three primary inputs: labor, capital, and imports.

If there is a single homogeneous primary factor a set of relative prices can be obtained. If three primary inputs are to replace the previous single primary input it is necessary to assume that each of the three is also homogeneous; that is, in addition to assuming a homogeneous labor force, imports are considered as a homogeneous unit, as is also capital.

Again under long-run perfectly competitive conditions, the equilibrium price for each producible output must be equal to its unit cost which will consist of the costs per unit of each intermediate input plus the direct costs associated with the inputs of labor, capital, and imports. Reformulating (14) to include the additional primary factors we have

$$P_j = m_jP_m + k_jP_k + f_jP_f + \sum_{i=1}^{m} a_{ij}P_i \qquad (j = 1, 2, \ldots, m) \quad (24)$$

where m_j represents the required amount of imports per unit of output of the jth industry; P_m, a uniform price of imports; k_j, the amount of capital absorbed by the jth industry per unit of its output; and P_k, a uniform rate of interest.

We may consider the product of the import coefficients, m_j $(j = 1, 2, \ldots, m)$, and a uniform price of imports, P_m, to form constants, M_j $(j = 1, 2, \ldots, m)$, and the product of the capital input coefficients, k_j $(j = 1, 2, \ldots, m)$, and some uniform rate of interest which we will assume to be a relative rate of interest, the determination of which will be dealt with later, to form constants K_j $(j = 1, 2, \ldots, m)$. Thus expressing $(m_j)(P_m)$, the product of the required amount of imports per unit of output of the jth industry and the price of imports as constants M_j $(j = 1, 2, \ldots, m)$ and $(k_j)(P_k)$ the product of the required amount of capital per unit of output of the jth industry and the rate of interest as constants K_j $(j = 1, 2, \ldots, m)$, (24) can be written as follows

$$P_j = M_j + K_j + f_jP_f + \sum_{i=1}^{m} a_{ij}P_i \qquad (j = 1, 2, \ldots, m) \qquad (25)$$

Again, it is impossible to solve for determinate prices of all

$m + 1$ variables. However, by choosing as numeraire P_f and expressing all other prices in terms of it, we can write the following linear nonhomogeneous set of equations to determine the m unknown price ratios

$$
\begin{aligned}
P'_1 &= M'_1 + K'_1 + f_1 + a_{11}P'_1 + a_{21}P'_2 + \ldots + a_{i1}P'_i + \ldots + a_{m1}P'_m \\
P'_2 &= M'_2 + K'_2 + f_2 + a_{12}P'_1 + a_{22}P'_2 + \ldots + a_{i2}P'_i + \ldots + a_{m2}P'_m \\
&\cdots \\
P'_i &= M'_i + K'_i + f_i + a_{1i}P'_i + a_{2i}P'_2 + \ldots + a_{ii}P'_i + \ldots + a_{mi}P'_m \\
&\cdots \\
P'_m &= M'_m + K'_m + f_m + a_{1m}P'_1 + a_{2m}P'_2 + \ldots + a_{im}P'_i + \ldots + a_{mm}P'_m
\end{aligned}
\qquad (26)
$$

where $P'_i = \frac{P_i}{P_f}$, $M'_i = \frac{M_i}{P_f}$, and $K'_i = \frac{K_i}{P_f}$ $(i = 1, 2, \ldots, m)$.

In matrix form

$$
\begin{bmatrix} P'_1 \\ P'_2 \\ \vdots \\ P'_i \\ \vdots \\ P'_m \end{bmatrix}
=
\begin{bmatrix} M'_1 \\ M'_2 \\ \vdots \\ M'_i \\ \vdots \\ M'_m \end{bmatrix}
+
\begin{bmatrix} K'_1 \\ K'_2 \\ \vdots \\ K'_i \\ \vdots \\ K'_m \end{bmatrix}
+
\begin{bmatrix} f_1 \\ f_2 \\ \vdots \\ f_i \\ \vdots \\ f_m \end{bmatrix}
+
\begin{bmatrix}
a_{11}a_{21} & \ldots & a_{i1} & \ldots & a_{m1} \\
a_{12}a_{22} & \ldots & a_{i2} & \ldots & a_{m2} \\
\cdots \\
a_{1i}a_{2i} & \ldots & a_{ii} & \ldots & a_{mi} \\
\cdots \\
a_{1m}a_{2m} & \ldots & a_{im} & \ldots & a_{mm}
\end{bmatrix}
\begin{bmatrix} P'_1 \\ P'_2 \\ \vdots \\ P'_i \\ \vdots \\ P'_m \end{bmatrix}
\qquad (27)
$$

or

$$P' = M' + K' + F + A_T P' \qquad (28)$$

which can be solved for the unknown relative prices

$$P' = (I - A)_T^{-1} M' + (I - A)_T^{-1} K' + (I - A)_T^{-1} F \qquad (29)$$

In the case of a single homogeneous primary input the set of relative prices is determined exclusively by the technological or structural parameters of the system. This, however, is not the case when additional primary factors are incorporated into the equation system. The inclusion of two additional primary factors, such as the above suggests, creates a system which involves more variables than equations; by choosing the price of any one of the three primary factors as numeraire and expressing all other prices in terms of it, we are left with

m equations to determine $m + 2$ unknown relative prices. We cannot, therefore, hope to solve for determinate price ratios of all $m + 2$ variables unless it is possible to consider two of the prices—here it is natural to consider the prices of the two additional primary inputs—as determined outside the system. That is, by determining the prices of the remaining two primary inputs exogenously the system is reduced to m equations in m unknowns and is thus determinate. However, unlike the case of a single homogeneous primary factor, the resulting set of relative prices is not determined entirely by the structural parameters of the system, but by the exogenously determined prices as well. Since in the current framework P_f, the price of labor, is chosen as numeraire, the price of imports, P_m, and the rate of interest, P_k, which is applied to capital, are considered exogenous and enter into the determination of the relative prices, P_i/P_f $(i = 1, 2, \ldots, m)$.

$$\begin{aligned} P'_j = {} & (A_{1j}M'_1 + A_{2j}M'_2 + \ldots + A_{mj}M'_m) \\ & + (A_{1j}K'_1 + A_{2j}K'_2 + \ldots + A_{mj}K'_m) \\ & + (A_{1j}f_1 + A_{2j}f_2 + \ldots + A_{mj}f_m) \\ & (j = 1, 2, \ldots, m) \end{aligned} \tag{30}$$

where

$$P'_j = \frac{P_j}{P_f}, \quad M'_j = \frac{(m_j)\,(P_m)}{P_f},$$

$$\text{and } K'_j = \frac{(k_j)\,(P_k)}{P_f} \quad (j = 1, 2, \ldots, m).$$

As shown previously, much of the theoretical development of input-output analysis is premised upon a labor theory of value. For example, the substitution theorem, originally proved for an open static system, while establishing that there is one preferred set of input ratios independent of the bill of final consumption, assumes that labor is the sole primary factor or "nonproduced good." It is interesting to have rigorous demonstrations of such theorems, but we may question their value except as a step toward coordinating theorems for a world in which there is more than one scarce resource. Clearly, the inclusion of three primary factors sets our analysis apart from a labor theory of value. The total labor costs of say the jth output no longer equals P_j/P_f, the competitively determined price of the jth good relative to the wage rate, as is the case when labor is the sole primary input (30).

We have thus far arrived at a set of relative prices, P_i/P_f ($i = 1, 2, \ldots, m$), which are determined jointly by the structural parameters and the exogenously determined price variables. The objective of the analysis is to generate, within the above framework, price data which can be compared with actual or observed price data to determine the relative structural stability of the system over time. Therefore, it is necessary to eliminate insofar as possible the effects of the exogenously determined variables on the price structure thus generated; that is, to arrive at a price structure which is determined by technological relationships only. If the above framework is used to generate price data at time t and again at time $t + 1$ (the base period), and if the values of the exogenous variables are determined separately for each point in time the following sets of price data (31) and (32) can be calculated:

$$P''(t+1) = [(I - A)_T^{-1} M'(t+1) + (I - A)_T^{-1} K'(t+1) + (I - A)_T^{-1} F(t+1)]\, P_f(t+1) \tag{31}$$

where

$$M'_j(t+1) = \frac{m_j(t+1)\, P_m(t+1)}{P_f(t+1)} \quad (j = 1, 2, \ldots, m),$$

$$K'_j(t+1) = \frac{k_j(t+1)\, P_k(t+1)}{P_f(t+1)} \quad (j = 1, 2, \ldots, m)$$

and where $P_f(t + 1)$ and $P''(t + 1)$ represent, respectively, the wage rate (a scalar) and the vector of absolute price levels at time $t + 1$.

Previously the system yielded a set of prices all of which were expressed relative to a numeraire. Therefore by multiplying the relative prices by the numeraire the absolute price levels are obtained. In (31) this amounts to multiplying the expression in brackets—the sum of three $m \times 1$ vectors—by the wage rate; the numeraire in terms of which all other prices are expressed.

$$P''(t) = [(I - A)_T^{-1} M'(t) + (I - A)_T^{-1} K'(t) + (I - A)_T^{-1} F(t + 1)]\, P_f(t) \qquad (32)$$

where

$$M'_j(t) = \frac{m_j(t+1)\, P_m(t)}{P_f(t)} \qquad (j = 1, 2, \ldots, m),$$

$$K'_j(t) = \frac{k_j(t+1)\, P_k(t)}{P_f(t)} \qquad (j = 1, 2, \ldots, m)$$

and where $P_f(t)$ and $P''(t)$ represent, respectively, the wage rate and the vector of absolute price levels at time t.

In converting relative prices to absolute prices, the wage rate is entered as another exogenously determined value. By calculating a wage rate, an import price index, and a rate of interest at time t and again at time $t + 1$, any variation in the price structure generated within the system for each of the two points in time depends upon and is determined by variations in the structural parameters.

In order to establish whether a given set of input coefficients remained stable (were invariant) over the period of time t to $t + 1$, we can, by calculating $P''(t)$ and $P''(t + 1)$ and by forming the ratio $P''_i(t + 1)/P''_i(t)$ $(i = 1, 2, \ldots, m)$ for each sector included in the system, compare these ratios with the ratios of the actual price indices, $P_i(t + 1)/P_i(t)$ $(i = 1, 2, \ldots, m)$, corresponding to each of the sectors. A necessary condition[2] then for the invariance of a given set of

[2]Let S and $\overline{S}$ refer to time $t + 1$ (the base period) and t respectively, and let $a = (I - A)_T^{-1}$. Then equation (31) can be written:

$$P = P'' = a(mP'_m + kP'_k + F)P_f$$

where P is a vector of observed prices (observed and calculated prices for a given time period must be equal) and P'_m and P'_k are the scalars P_m/P_f and P_k/P_f respectively. Correspondingly we have:

$$\overline{P} = \overline{a}(\overline{mP'_m} + \overline{kP'_k} + \overline{F})\overline{P}_f$$

Equation (32) then becomes

$$\overline{P''} = a(m\overline{P'}_m + k\overline{P'}_k + F)\overline{P}_f$$

Since $P'' = P$ the critical equality, $\overline{P''}/\overline{P''} = P/\overline{P}$, is equivalent to $\overline{P''} = \overline{P}$ or $a(m\overline{P'}_m + k\overline{P'}_k + F)\overline{P}_f = \overline{a}(\overline{mP'_m} + \overline{kP'_k} + \overline{F})\overline{P}_f$, which in turn is

Continued next page

coefficients over time is that the observed and calculated price ratios be equal; that is

$$P''_i(t+1)/P''_i(t) = P_i(t+1)/P_i(t) \qquad i = 1, 2, \ldots, m$$

If, therefore, $P''_i(t+1)/P''_i(t)$ is plotted on the vertical and $P_i(t+1)/P_i(t)$ on the horizontal axis of a two variable plane a necessary condition for stability is met when the observed points lie on or cluster about a 45 degree straight line through the origin. A wide divergent scatter, on the other hand, implies that the input structure underwent change.

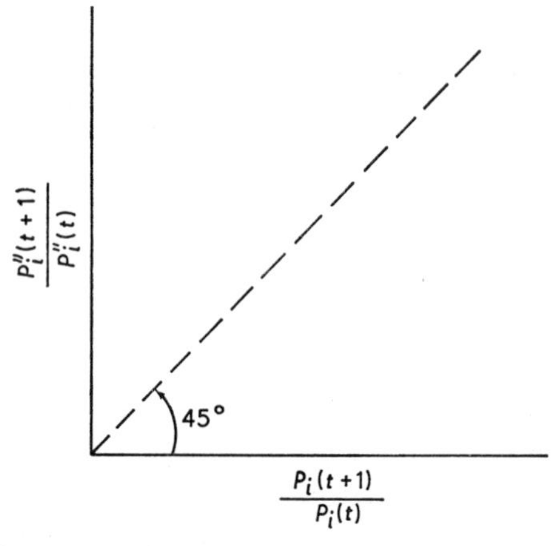

In general, we would hardly expect the observed points to coincide with the straight 45 degree line. However, the stronger the tendency for the scatter to converge to the 45 degree line, the less the technical or structural parameters of the system varied, while on the other hand, the stronger the tendency for the scatter to diverge from the 45 degree line, the greater the variation or change in the technological parameters.

---

equivalent to $(am - \overline{am})\overline{P}'_m + (ak - \overline{ak})\overline{P}'_k + (aF - \overline{aF}) = O$, where $\overline{P}'_m$ and $\overline{P}'_k$ are scalars. Therefore, unchanged technology ($a = \overline{a}$, $m = \overline{m}$, $k = \overline{k}$, $F = \overline{F}$) implies the equality $P''/\overline{P}'' = P/\overline{P}$; on the other hand, this equality does not imply unchanged technology, but merely the disappearance of the bracketed vectors in the above relationship. That is, $P''/\overline{P}'' = P/\overline{P}$ is a necessary but not sufficient condition for unchanged technology.

Transformation of Structural Coefficients

The pure theory of input-output analysis suggests a method for explaining a wide range of economic phenomena in terms of a basic matrix of coefficients describing the technological interdependence of the industries comprising the economy. The main interest in such a system is not, however, its descriptive value relating to some base year, but in the inferences which can be drawn from it regarding past, current, or future time periods. That is, the structural matrix will typically be used to estimate the probable impact throughout the economy of a different set of end-product deliveries or production schedules from those which prevailed in the base year. This necessarily requires that the technical parameters of the system remain invariant over time. Since, however, most progressive economic systems are in a constant state of change, it is reasonable to assume that the "fact of change" cannot be wholly ignored and then proceed to establish whether or not shifts in input patterns for some relevant time period occurred. We have already defined a systematic scheme based on the comparison of prices generated within the open system with actual or observed prices to establish the existence or nonexistence, whichever the case may be, of shifted input patterns; that is, changes in the structural parameters of the system.

If the empirical results of such an analysis reveal substantial changes or shifts in input patterns for the time period under study, is it possible to begin with the cross-sectional analysis for the base year, say $t + 1$, and, by using it as a bench mark, effect adjustments which would transform the technological structure of that year back to, say, that of year t?[3]

[3]The question might well have been concerned with transforming technology forward from some given base year t to, say, some year in the future $t + 1$. However, since the analysis of the Finnish economy requires knowledge of the structural parameters for the year 1952, it is necessary to "back cast" since the base year for the only input-output study available is 1956.

Even with fully detailed and accurate structural information for the base year this is likely to be no small undertaking.

It has traditionally been the case, where the input-output technique has been used to bring additional information to bear on the problem of economic analysis, that new and revised tabulations of the data have been made periodically in order to keep the basic tables up to date. However, where statistical information is not sufficiently detailed and accurate to permit the compilation of a revised or completely new set of technical coefficients which comprise the structural matrix of the system, it appears that some adjustment of the existing matrix must be attempted. Such an adjustment must be based on a hypothesis which is directed at explaining the movement in the structural parameters. It could be used to transform the technological relationships of the base year to represent technology as it existed in some year other than the base year. If projections based on such an adjusted structural matrix could be shown to be more accurate in some sense than those based on the original matrix, such an adjustment might have rather wide practical application as well as theoretical interest.

The following discussion suggests one of the many possible adjustments or transformations which might be performed on the structural coefficients of the base year. This particular transformation is not necessarily more effective, empirically, than other transformations. In fact, since it is not unique, it must be made clear that whether or not the transformed technological structure more closely approximates the true structure is a matter to be determined empirically. Through this particular transformation, however, we acquire a technological structure for a given year, different from the base year, which, in the case under study, does more closely approximate the true structure or structure which actually existed in that year than does the technical or structural matrix of the base year. That is, empirical computations based on the transformed input-output coefficients are for the case considered more accurate than those based on the coefficients of the original matrix. Inherent in the latter is the assumption that the structure of the system remained invariant between the base year and the year under study.

All practical applications of the input-output technique as developed in recent years follow the open pattern, which omits from the theoretically complete set of structural coefficients some of those which connect, for example, consumer and governmental purchases with the other parts of the system. The actual magnitudes of these particular kinds of inputs are fixed by prescribing a specific "bill of goods" constituting what in this context is called the final demand; then through theoretical computations—which amount to the solution of a large system of simultaneous linear equations—the structurally necessary magnitudes of all the remaining inputs and outputs can be determined. However, in order to make the following transformation consistent with theory it becomes necessary to consider the system as closed; that is, the system must be self-contained. For example, foreign trade, government, households, and so on are all considered to be industries. Households consume various commodities and produce labor and entrepreneurial services, foreign trade consumes exports and produces imports, and government supplies goods and services and buys part of each industry's output. Such a system itself can be regarded as being a part of a still more comprehensive system containing structural stock-flow relationships and so on. Thus the idea of closure is to be considered as a relative concept.

Beginning with an open model such as

$$X_i = \sum_{j=1}^{m} x_{ij} + Y_i \qquad (i = 1, 2, \ldots, m) \qquad (33)$$

if the Ys are considered as variables we may conveniently label them with the previously used symbol x_{in} so that (33) becomes

$$X_i = \sum_{j=1}^{n} x_{ij} \qquad (i = 1, 2, \ldots, n) \qquad (34)$$

where $n = m + 1$. Thus the nth rows and columns have been adjoined to the system. Substituting the technological relationship $x_{ij} = a_{ij}X_j$ $(i, j = 1, 2, \ldots, n)$ into (34) and expressing it in matrix form we have

$$X = AX \tag{35}$$

where A is the matrix of technical coefficients and X the column vector of output levels. We have already seen the "duality" relation between quantities and prices, so that by transposing the A matrix in the quantity problem of (35) we arrive at the corresponding price problem

$$P = A_T P \tag{36}$$

where P is a column vector of prices. As was noted in a previous section, in order for a nontrivial solution to exist for equations (35) and (36) the determinant of the identity matrix minus the coefficient matrix must vanish. Stated slightly differently, the homogeneous equations

$$(I - A)X = \theta \tag{37}$$

$$(I - A_T)P = \theta \tag{38}$$

have nonzero solutions only when the rank of $(I - A)$ in the case of the former, and of $(I - A_T)$ in the case of the latter, is less than n, that is, when $(I - A)$, to consider only the former, is singular, one of its columns can be expressed as a linear combination of the others, which is the same thing as saying that a nontrivial combination of the columns can be made equal to the null vector, $(I - A)\,\overline{X} = \theta$, for $\overline{X} \neq \theta$. However, if $\overline{X}$ represents a solution, $k\overline{X}$, for any scalar k, will likewise represent a solution. Thus the closed input-output equations described do not determine the levels, but rather the structure of prices and outputs.

If, however, in the closed system, every industry sells to the final consumption sector and if every industry purchases labor, capital, or imports, both A and A_T are irreducible.[4] For

[4]An nth-order matrix, A, is called reducible if by interchanging rows and corresponding columns it is possible to obtain the form

$$A = \begin{bmatrix} A_{11} & A_{12} \\ 0 & A_{22} \end{bmatrix}$$

Continued next page

the present problem this means that, to the "maximal" characteristic value of A and of A_T there corresponds a characteristic vector with positive coordinates.[5] Let X, the vector of output levels and P, the vector of prices, be the positive vectors corresponding to the "maximal" characteristic value of A and A_T respectively. If, then, we observe changes in either the price structure, P, or the output structure, X, it is assumed that the technical parameters comprising A have changed. Thus we come to the basic hypothesis underlying the suggested transformation. That is, if changes in the structural matrix A are considered to be reflected in the price structure, the price structure may then be used as a basis for effecting adjustments on the technical parameters to compensate for such changes.

Expressing both vectors and matrices as functions of time

$$X(t) = A(t)\,X(t) \tag{39}$$

$$P(t) = A_T(t)\,P(t) \tag{40}$$

we may examine the system at time t and again at time $t + 1$. Both $P(t)$ and $P(t + 1)$ are vectors with positive components. Therefore we can find a nonsingular matrix D such that

$$P(t + 1) = D\,P(t) \tag{41}$$

---

where A_{11} and A_{22} are square matrices. Otherwise A is called irreducible. If A_{11}, A_{22} in the foregoing expression are reducible, A assumes the form

$$A = \begin{bmatrix} A_1 & A_{12} \dots A_{1k} \\ 0 & A_2 \dots A_{2k} \\ \dots & \dots \\ 0 & 0 \dots A_k \end{bmatrix}$$

where $A_1, A_2, \dots, A_k$ are square irreducible matrices. See F. R. Gantmacher, *The Theory of Matrices*, Vol. 2 (New York: Chelsea Publishing Company, 1959), pp. 50, 75.

[5]Theorem: "An irreducible non-negative matrix A always has a positive characteristic value r that is a simple root of the characteristic equation. The moduli of all the other characteristic values do not exceed r. To the 'maximal' characteristic value r there corresponds a characteristic vector with positive coordinates." (See Gantmacher, *op. cit.*, p. 53.)

There are presumably many matrices which will transform $P(t)$ into $P(t+1)$. Of these, a particularly simple one is the diagonal matrix, having as its ith diagonal element $P_i(t+1)/P_i(t)$. Rewriting (40) for time $t+1$ and making use of the relationship in (41) we get the following

$$P(t+1) = A_T(t+1)\,P(t+1)$$

$$DP(t) = A_T(t+1)\,DP(t) \tag{42}$$

and

$$P(t) = [D^{-1}A_T(t+1)\,D]P(t) \tag{43}$$

Since $P(t) = A_T(t)P(t)$, set

$$A_T(t) = [D^{-1}A_T(t+1)\,D] \tag{44}$$

Taking the transpose of the expression in brackets in (43) we get the corresponding quantity problem

$$X(t) = [D_T A(t+1)\,D_T^{-1}]\,X(t) \tag{45}$$

Since $X(t) = A(t)X(t)$, set[6]

$$A(t) = [D_T A(t+1)\,D_T^{-1}] \tag{46}$$

which represents the desired transformation.

Since D is the diagonal matrix of price ratios, $d_{ii} = P_i(t+1)/P_i(t)$, multiplying the structural matrix of the base year, $A(t+1)$, on the right by D^{-1} and on the left by D implies that all the diagonal elements of the transformed structural matrix, $A(t)$, will be the same as those of the original matrix and that the off diagonal elements will be of the form

$$[P_j(t)/P_j(t+1)\;P_i(t+1)/P_i(t)]\,a_{ij} \tag{47}$$

$$(i, j = 1, 2, \ldots, n)$$

where the as are the coefficients of $A(t+1)$.

This simple hypothesis is sufficient to transform an input-output matrix of some base year $t+1$ into a matrix which is consistent with the price structure actually existing at some earlier year t. It is thus possible to use this matrix to answer

[6] Professor E. Ames develops this adjustment technique in a manuscript entitled *Linear Economics*. There, however, the adjustment process is not limited to the diagonal matrix.

the problem encountered in applying input-output analysis to the postwar economy of Finland in which the only available input-output study is based on 1956 technology.

Even though the transformation thus described may be consistent with theory, the fact that it relies entirely on price ratios corresponding to the various sectors of the system implies that its domain of accurate adjustment may be rather narrow. That is, such a transformation can hardly be expected to account for all the shifts or changes in input patterns which may have occurred. It is further recognized that failure to correct for these shifted patterns will affect the results or computations in proportion to their importance.

Since the diagonal matrix D is not the only matrix which would effect the observed changes in price, its real value at this stage will necessarily be determined by detailed empirical investigation; that is, the usefulness of the suggested transformation depends upon empirical validation. (In a subsequent section it will be shown that the transformed 1956 structural matrix combined with the 1952 final bill of demand yields a set of production levels which more closely approximate the true 1952 levels than those based on the untransformed 1956 structural matrix.)

The general theoretical scheme outlined above is designed to absorb and to exploit for analytical purposes a large amount of detailed factual information. However, caution should be taken against the careless assumption that simple possession of the interindustry relations data leads to quick and easy solutions for important problems.

5

EMPIRICAL APPLICATION

The previous two chapters have shown that the effect of reparations on the Finnish economy is a topic which can be formulated in terms of the interindustrial relations concepts of the input-output model. To apply this model to Finnish data, it will now be necessary to consider whether in fact the technology of the Finnish economy remained constant during the 1950s. If, as one might expect, it did not, it is necessary to show that the changes in the structure of the Finnish account can actually be represented by the transformation described in the preceding chapter.

An interindustry study of reparations, beginning with the armistice of 1944 and extending through the completion of payments, in September, 1952, requires a wealth of detailed factual information which we do not have at our disposal at the present time. We do have, however, the input-output structure of the Finnish economy for the year 1956, plus sufficient data describing the price structure for the period 1952–56, to determine whether input patterns shifted (whether there was structural instability) and to effect a compensating transformation. That is, available data apart from the reparation payments per se permit us to establish a check on the stability of the technical parameters between 1952 and 1956 and to compensate for structural changes by effecting a transformation on the 1956 structure, a_{ij}s, to approximate the structure existing in 1952. For periods extending beyond 1952, however, adequate data are not available. Thus, even though a complete interindustry study of the indemnity implies structural knowledge for each year of payments, the present inquiry will necessarily be limited to approximating, through the previously outlined procedure, the input-output structure for 1952, the final year of payments only. Inherent in this limitation is the assumption that all indemnity deliveries—goods delivered to the Soviet Union under the indemnity account—were produced with the technical structure that existed in 1952.

The following discussion will be concerned with (1) calculating within the framework of the open static system a price structure to be compared with the observed price structure in establishing the existence of shifted input patterns for the period under study, 1952–56; (2) effecting a compensating transformation; and (3) showing that the transformed structural matrix more closely approximates the true 1952 structure than does the original 1956 matrix which implies no change in the input parameters.

Structural Stability of the Finnish Economy Between 1952 and 1956

Basic to the generation of prices within the framework of the open static input-output system is the assumption of long-run competitive equilibrium where profits have been eliminated and where all primary inputs within the respective divisions—labor, capital, and imports—are assumed homogeneous with a uniform price. Under such perfectly competitive "statical" conditions, the equilibrium price of each producible good will equal its unit cost of production which consists of costs per unit of each intermediate input, plus direct costs associated with the inputs of labor, capital, and imports. Thus for the output (product) of each of the 39 sectors included in the Finnish input-output study, the following conditions hold

$$P_j = m_j P_m + k_j P_k + f_j P_f + \sum_{i=1}^{39} a_{ij} P \qquad (48)$$
$$(j = 1, 2, \ldots, 39)$$

where, as indicated previously, m_j, k_j, and f_j represent the required amounts of imports, capital, and labor, respectively, per unit of output of the jth industry, and where P_m represents the price of imports, P_k the rate of interest,[1] and P_f the wage rate.

The first two terms on the right of (48), $(m_j)(P_m)$ and $(k_j)(P_k)$, may be expressed as constants M_j and K_j ($j = 1, 2, \ldots, 39$) which implies that the coefficients, m_j, k_j, along with the price of imports and the rate of interest, are known —determined exogenously. Although the input coefficients (obtained from the input-output table) and the price of imports (import price index) are readily available, a rate of interest, P_k, which can be applied to the k_js in establishing the value added to per unit costs of the jth output as a result of the required capital input is somewhat vague and difficult to define. However, the following suggests a relationship from which it is possible to derive a suitable rate of interest.[2]

Denote the price of a new capital good k by P_k and the rate of interest by r. If we let $\mu_k P_k$ and $v_k P_k$ ($k = 1, 2, \ldots, n$) be the proportions representing, respectively, the depreciation charges and the insurance premiums to be deducted from the gross income, p_k, of the capital good k, we have the equation

$$P_k = \frac{p_k}{r + \mu_k + v_k} \qquad (k = 1, 2, \ldots, n) \qquad (49)$$

Denoting, for simplicity, $(\mu_k + v_k)$ by q_k we can express the above equation as

$$P_k = \frac{p_k}{r + q_k} \qquad (k = 1, 2, \ldots, n) \qquad (50)$$

[1]The term "rate of interest" as used here applies to the rate of return on property. Finnish statistics separate labor income from property income, and this discussion is an attempt to derive a statistical connection between property and the income of its owners in Finland. Theorists of the rate of interest will recognize the extent to which the discussion, from a theoretical point of view, has been abbreviated.

[2]L. Walras, *Elements of Pure Economics* (Homewood, Illinois: Richard D. Irwin, Inc., 1954), p. 275.

Originally r represented the rate of net income which is the ratio of the net price of capital service to the price of the capital good, but the rate of net income tends to coincide with the monetary rate of interest.[3]

If capital is homogeneous, P_k can be considered as a uniform price of capital—a single price that can be applied to capital in general since all units of capital are assumed alike; p_k as gross income per unit of capital; and q_k as the rate of depreciation on capital; with r representing a uniform rate of interest. Therefore, by expressing (50) as $p_k = P_k\ (r + q_k)$ and multiplying both sides by Q, (the total physical volume of capital) we arrive at the expression

$$Qp_k = QP_k r + QP_k q_k \tag{51}$$

where Qp_k, the physical volume of capital times per unit gross income and $Q(P_k q_k)$, the physical volume of capital times the per unit depreciation charge, correspond to income from property and depreciation, respectively, from the national income accounts. Denoting, for simplicity, Qp_k by IP and $Q(P_k q_k)$ by D and solving for $QP_k r$ equation (51) can be written as

$$QP_k r = IP - D \tag{52}$$

If an expression such as (52) is formulated for each of two time periods, t and $t + 1$, and expressed as a ratio of $t + 1$ to t, it is possible to infer a relative rate of interest that can be applied in determining the unknown price ratios in (48)

$$\frac{QP_k r(t + 1)}{QP_k r(t)} = \frac{(IP(t + 1) - D(t + 1)\ )}{(IP(t) - D(t)\ )} \tag{53}$$

Since QP_k, the value of fixed plant and equipment for an entire economy, is not available, assume that its value in time $t + 1$ relative to its value in time t is proportional to depreciation in time $t + 1$ relative to depreciation in time t. That is, assume that

$$\frac{QP_k(t + 1)}{QP_k(t)} = \frac{D(t + 1)}{D(t} \tag{54}$$

[3] *Ibid.*, pp. 289–90.

Therefore

$$\frac{QP_k r(t+1)}{QP_k r(t)} = \frac{QP_k(t+1)}{QP_k(t)} \cdot \frac{r(t+1)}{r(t)} = \frac{D(t+1)}{D(t)} \cdot \frac{r(t+1)}{r(t)} \quad (55)$$

Substituting the above into (53) and solving for $r(t+1)/r(t)$ we have

$$\frac{r(t+1)}{r(t)} = \frac{(IP(t+1) - D(t+1))}{(IP(t) - D(t))} \cdot \frac{D(t)}{D(t+1)} \quad (56)$$

Since the object of the current analysis is to determine the structural stability of the Finnish economy between 1952, (t), and 1956, $(t+1)$, a rate of interest for the latter year relative to that of the former will suffice for comparative purposes.

Given equation system (48) with the technical coefficients of both intermediate and primary inputs, the rate of interest which is assumed to be a relative rate of interest, the price of imports and the wage rate specified, the absolute level of prices corresponding to the individual sectors contained within the system are determined for each of the years 1952 and 1956 as follows:

$$\begin{aligned} P''(56) = [&(I-A)_T^{-1}M' + (I-A)_T^{-1}K'(56) \\ &+ (I-A)_T^{-1}F(56)]\, P_f(56) \end{aligned} \quad (57)$$

where

$$M_j'(56) = \frac{m_j(56)P_m(56)}{P_f(56)} \qquad (j = 1, 2, \ldots, 39)$$

$$K_j'(56) = \frac{k_j(56)P_k(56)}{P_f(56)} \qquad (j = 1, 2, \ldots, 39)$$

and where $P_f(56)$ and $P''(56)$ represent, respectively, the wage rate and the vector of absolute prices which prevailed in 1956.

$$\begin{aligned} P''(52) = [&(I-A)_T^{-1}M'(52) + (I-A)_T^{-1}K'(52) \\ &+ (I-A)_T^{-1}F(56)]\, P_f(52) \end{aligned} \quad (58)$$

where

$$M_j'(52) = \frac{m_j(56)P_m(52)}{P_f(52)} \qquad (j = 1, 2, \ldots, 39)$$

$$K_j'(52) = \frac{k_j(56)P_k(52)}{P_f(52)} \qquad (j = 1, 2, \ldots, 39)$$

and where $P_f(52)$ and $P''(52)$ represent, respectively, the wage rate and the vector of absolute prices which prevailed in 1952.

If changes within the structural matrix are reflected in the price structure, any differences between the calculated price changes, $P''_i(56)/P''_i(52)$ $(i = 1, 2, \ldots, 39)$, and the corresponding observed price changes $P_i(56)/P_i(52)$ $(i = 1, 2, \ldots, 39)$, imply changes within the structural makeup of the system; that is, changes in the input-output matrix.

FIGURE 5–1

CALCULATED AND OBSERVED PRICE RATIOS

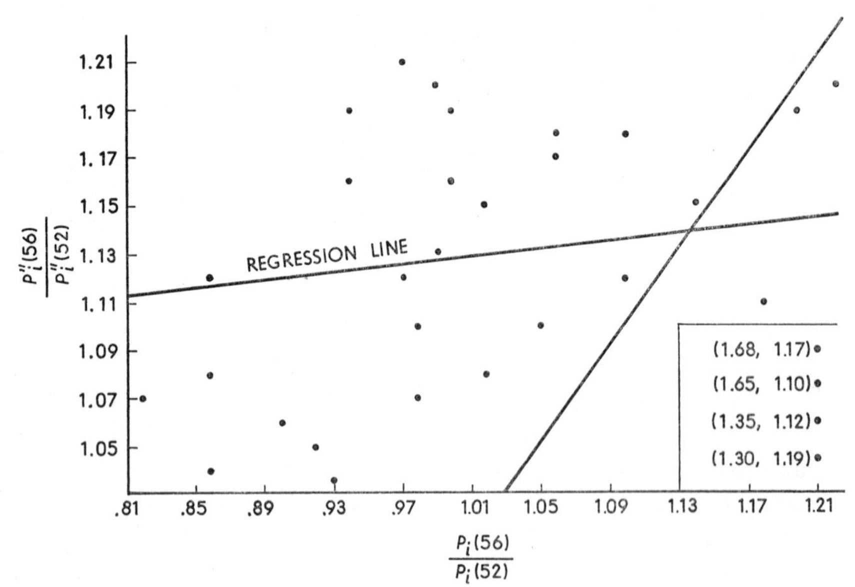

SOURCE: Table 5–1.

Figure 5–1 and Table 5–1 compare the calculated price changes, $P''_i(56)/P''_i(52)$, with the observed price changes, $P_i(56)/P_i(52)$, for the Finnish economy. As might well be ex-

TABLE 5-1

RATIOS OF 1956 TO 1952 PRICES BY SECTORS

Sectors	Calculated Price Ratios $P''_i(56)/P''_i(52)$	Observed Price Ratios $P''_i(56)/P_i(52)$
1. Agriculture	1.18	1.10
2. Hunting and fishing	1.20	1.22
3. Forestry	1.21	.97
4. Mining and quarrying	1.15	1.14
5. Food manufacturing industries	1.12	1.10
6. Beverage industries	1.12	—
7. Tobacco manufactures	1.05	.92
8. Manufacture of textiles	1.07	.82
9. Manufacture of footwear, other wearing apparel, and made-up textile goods	1.12	.86
10. Manufacture of wood and cork, except manufacture of furniture	1.19	1.00
11. Manufacture of furniture and fixtures	1.17	1.68
12. Manufacture of paper and paper products	1.16	1.00
13. Printing, publishing, and allied industries	1.19	.94
14. Manufacture of leather and leather products, except footwear	1.08	.86
15. Manufacture of rubber products	1.08	1.02
16. Manufacture of chemicals and chemical products	1.04	.86
17. Manufacture of products of petroleum and asphalt	1.03	.93
18. Manufacture of nonmetallic mineral products	1.15	1.02
19. Basic metal industries	1.07	.98
20. Manufacture of metal products, except machinery and transport equipment	1.10	.98
21. Manufacture of machinery, except electrical machinery	1.12	.97
22. Manufacture of electrical machinery, apparatus, appliances, and supplies	1.10	1.65
23. Manufacture of transport equipment	1.11	1.18
24. Miscellaneous industries	1.13	.99
25. House construction	1.17	1.06
26. Other construction	1.18	1.06
27. Electricity, gas, steam, and water services	1.10	1.05
28. Trade	1.20	.99
29. Banking and insurance	1.12	1.35
30. Railway transport	1.16	.94
31. Tramway and bus transport	1.15	—
32. Other road transport	1.17	—
33. Water transport	1.06	.90
34. Air transport	1.09	—
35. Services incidental to transportation	1.19	—
36. Communication	1.19	1.20
37. Central government	1.18	—
38. Local authorities	1.19	1.30
39. Other services	1.19	—

SOURCE: Calculated by author from figures provided by Central Statistical Office of Finland.

pected there is a wide divergence between the observed price changes and price changes which would have occurred if the 1956 input-output matrix had prevailed in 1952. The technological structure of the Finnish economy as defined by a set of input-output coefficients cannot, therefore, be considered as having remained invariant for the period under study, 1952–56. In Figure 5–1 $P''_i(56)/P''_i(52)$ and $P_i(56)/P_i(52)$ are plotted respectively on the vertical and horizontal axis of a two-variable plane. The scatter does not converge to the 45 degree line, which would indicate relative stability of the input-output matrix. There is instead a marked scatter, which means that the input structure underwent substantial change.[4]

Thus, even though the period 1952–56 is short the changes in the input-output matrix seem to have been significant from the point of view of prediction. In this sense, the criterion proposed for invariance of the studies cited above[5]—changes

---

[4]Calculated prices in Figure 5–1 and Table 5–1 are based on the 1956 technical coefficients with the price of imports, the rate of interest, and the wage rate determined separately for each year 1952 and 1956 as follows: price of imports for 1952, 121, and for 1956, 105 (import price index, 1954 = 100); the wage rate for 1952, 136, and for 1956, 165 (average of all wage rates in marks per hour); and the rate of interest for 1952, 1.00, and for 1956, 1.70 (calculated according to the method outlined on pages 77–79 with 21.7 and 37.9 billion marks representing income from property in 1952 and 1956, respectively, and with 26.4 and 54.3 billion marks representing depreciation in 1952 and 1956, respectively. Both income from property and depreciation are taken from the national income accounts).

Observed prices in Figure 5–1 and Table 5–1 are acquired from a breakdown of the wholesale price index (1938 = 100). See Tilastollinen Päätoimisto, *Tilastokatsauksia,* XXX–1955, XXVI–1961, (Bulletin of Statistics, Central Statistical Office of Finland). For the sectors, banking and insurance and local authorities, for which there is no explicit price data, the price ratio estimates were based on average monthly earnings of all employees in banks and insurance companies in the case of the former and on average earnings per hour of municipal workers in the case of the latter. For seven of the sectors relevant data could not be obtained.

A straight line fitted to the points forming the scatter in Figure 5–1, $P''(56)/P''(52) = 1.0465 + .0793\ (P(56)/P(52))$, may be interpreted as indicating a general tendency or direction of movement; that is, calculated prices, with certain exceptions, rose slightly more between 1952 and 1956 than did observed prices. However, even though it is possible to find a linear function of best fit, the scatter is so wide and divergent that little meaning can be attached to it ($r^2 = .0918$).

[5]Clark, *op. cit.*, pp. 159–60.

of 20 percent in individual coefficients—may not be entirely relevant. It is not possible to determine how much the input-output coefficients changed in Finland from 1952 to 1956; however, they did change enough so that it is not possible to "back cast" the changes in Finnish prices for that period.

Transformation of the Structural Coefficients

Given that the technological structure of the Finnish economy between 1952 and 1956 underwent substantial change, the question arises as to whether it is possible to improve our backcasting ability by some theoretically suggested transformation of the input-output matrix. That is, the current objective must be to calculate and test a new matrix based on the hypothesis of the preceding chapter and to show that it more closely approximates the 1952 structure than does the original matrix, which assumes no change in the technical parameters.

In order to keep the proposed transformation consistent with input-output theory, it becomes necessary to "close" the original system of open equations; that is, adjoin to the input-output matrix the nth rows and columns which correspond to the value added sector and the final bill of demand, respectively.[6] Once closed, the system's price and quantity relationships can be expressed for each year 1952 and 1956 as follows:

[6]A system is said to be closed with respect to consumer demand, for example, if it contains equations describing the structural characteristics of the household sector—corresponding rows and columns in the input-output matrix. In the case of the Finnish model, closure implies that the columns comprising final demand—Gross capital formation, Consumption, Exports, and Undistributed—and the rows comprising value added—Labor income, Capital revenue, and Depreciation, Imports, and Indirect taxes minus subsidies, plus Undistributed—be added to the input-output matrix. Since, however, there is no direct corresponding entry in final demand for Labor income or Capital revenue plus Depreciation, and since there is no direct corresponding entry in the value added sector for Consumption or Gross capital formation, and so on, closure of the original open Finnish input-output model necessitates considering the four rows comprising value added and the four columns comprising final demand as forming a single row and a single column, respectively. In considering the interindustry flows, the row sum will then equal the column sum.

$$X(52) = A(52)X(52) \quad (59)$$

$$P(52) = A_T(52)P(52) \quad (60)$$

$$X(56) = A(56)X(56) \quad (61)$$

$$P(56) = A_T(56)P(56) \quad (62)$$

If changes within the structural makeup of the Finnish economy for the period considered are reflected in the corresponding price structure, the price structure logically forms a basis for effecting a transformation to compensate for such changes. Thus we derive the following:

$$P(56) = DP(52) \quad (63)$$

where D is chosen to be the diagonal matrix so that $d_{ii} = P_i(56)/P_i(52)$ $(i = 1, 2, \ldots, 39)$. If we substitute (63) into (62), rearrange terms

$$P(52) = [D^{-1}A_T(56)D]\, P(52) \quad (64)$$

and transpose the expression in brackets, the corresponding quantity problem is derived

$$X(52) = [D_T A(56) D_T^{-1}]\, X(52) \quad (65)$$

Since $X(52) = A(52)X(52)$, set

$$A(52) = [D_T A(56) D_T^{-1}] \quad (66)$$

which represents the desired transformation. The transformed structural matrix for the Finnish economy, 1956 a_{ij}s adjusted according to (66) are presented in Appendix Table B-4.

Accuracy of the Transformed Structural Coefficients

Even though it may be theoretically possible to effect a transformation on the structure of a given base year to represent the structure that existed in some year different from the base year—in this case 1952, the final year of indemnity payments—inherent in the analysis is the necessity to verify empirically that the transformed structural matrix does in fact more closely approximate the 1952 structure than does the structural matrix of the base year; that is, that empirical computations based on the transformed input-output coefficients will in general be more accurate than those based on the coefficients of the original matrix.

The resolution of this problem may be found in applying both the transformed and the original base year structural matrices to the 1952 final bill of demand and comparing the corresponding sets of output levels with the output levels that actually prevailed in 1952. If the transformed structure is in some sense a better approximation of the structure that prevailed in 1952 than the original base year structure, variations between output levels projected on the basis of the transformed matrix and the true 1952 output levels will be less than corresponding variations between output levels projected on the basis of the untransformed or the original base year matrix and the 1952 output levels. That is, recalling that

$$\overline{X}_i = \sum_{j=1}^{39} A_{ij}(52)\,Y_j(52) \qquad (i = 1, 2, \ldots, 39) \qquad (67)$$

where $\overline{X}_i$ $(i = 1, 2, \ldots, 39)$ is the actual or observed output levels for 1952, Y_j $(j = 1, 2, \ldots, 39)$, the 1952 final bill of demand, and $A_{ij}(52)$ $(i, j = 1, 2, \ldots, 39)$, the elements of the matrix $(I - A)^{-1}$ which would have prevailed in 1952 had it been possible to calculate such a matrix,[7] we may apply the base year structural matrix (1956) to the given 1952 final bill of demand to calculate a set of output levels as follows:

$$X_i' = \sum_{j=1}^{39} A_{ij}(56)\,Y_j(52) \qquad (i = 1, 2, \ldots, 39) \qquad (68)$$

Deducting (68) from (67) we arrive at

$$(X_i' - \overline{X}_i) = \sum_{j=1}^{39} (A_{ij}(56) - A_{ij}(52))\,Y_j(52) \qquad (69)$$

$$(i = 1, 2, \ldots, 39)$$

[7]It has already been emphasized that a structural matrix estimated from 1952 observations, due to insufficient data, is not available. However, both price and volume index numbers are available for all but six of the sectors included in the study. See *Tilastokatsauksia*, XXX–1955, XXVI–1961, Tilastollinen Päätoimisto. (Sectors 6, 11, 17, 31, 32, and 35 are excluded.) Therefore, given the production levels for 1956, price and volume indices for both 1952 and 1956 production levels, for 1952 $\overline{X}_i$ $(i = 1, 2, \ldots, 33)$ can be calculated.

which demonstrates the interesting relationship that deviations betwen total estimated output, X'_i, and total observed output, $\overline{X}_i$, can be conceived of as a linear combination of the differences between elements of the appropriate row in the inverse matrix, with final demand constituting a system of weights.

We may also apply the transformed structural matrix to the given 1952 final bill of demand to arrive at another set of output levels to be compared with observed 1952 output levels as follows:

$$X_i'' = \sum_{j=1}^{39} A_{ij}(\text{tranf})\, Y_j(52) \qquad (i = 1, 2, \ldots, 39) \qquad (70)$$

Deducting (70) from (67) we arrive at

$$(X_i'' - \overline{X}_i) = \sum_{j=1}^{39} (A_{ij}(\text{tranf}) - A_{ij}(52))\, Y_j(52) \qquad (71)$$

If the transformed matrix is a better approximation of the 1952 structure than is the untransformed or base year matrix we would expect

$$\sum_{i=1}^{39} (X_i' - \overline{X}_i)^2 > \sum_{i=1}^{39} (X_i'' - \overline{X}_i)^2 \qquad (72)$$

Empirical evidence presented in Table 5–2 indicates for the particular economy and transformation considered the sum of squared deviations between observed 1952 output levels and output levels projected on the basis of the transformed matrix to be substantially less than the sum of squared deviations between 1952 output levels and those projected on the basis of the untransformed or original base year matrix. That is, the transformation in (66) applied to the Finnish economy over the period considered validates the above inequality.

Further reference to Table 5–2 reveals that if sectors 3, 13, 15, 22, 23, and 29, for which the deviations between observed 1952 output levels and those based on the untransformed matrix are particularly large, are deleted from the analysis, the left term of (72), while substantially reduced, is still larger than the right term implying additional support

TABLE 5–2

Deviations Between Observed 1952 Output Levels and Those Projected on the Basis of Both the Transformed and the Untransformed Matrices

(Billions of Marks)

Sector Number*	$\bar{X}_i$	X'_i	X''_i	$(\bar{X}'_i - X_i)$	$(X''_i - \bar{X}_i)$
1	186.85	185.57	187.01	–1.28	.16
2	3.26	3.18	3.23	–.08	–.03
3	90.98	93.04	89.77	2.06	–1.21
4	6.38	5.63	6.23	–.75	–.15
5	150.68	151.59	151.57	.91	.89
6	—	7.24	7.22	—	—
7	4.85	4.85	4.85	0.00	0.00
8	45.11	46.02	44.73	.91	–.38
9	42.32	41.55	41.38	–.77	–.94
10	69.72	70.36	68.88	.64	–.84
11	—	11.13	12.95	—	—
12	93.58	92.87	92.79	–.71	–.79
13	23.87	21.71	23.65	–2.16	–.22
14	5.54	5.31	5.27	–.23	–.27
15	6.75	6.95	7.10	.20	.35
16	28.38	31.11	27.37	2.73	–1.01
17	—	1.68	1.64	—	—
18	19.60	18.74	18.25	–.86	–1.35
19	27.22	27.81	26.59	.59	–.63
20	18.88	19.18	18.36	.30	–.52
21	36.26	36.88	35.99	.62	–.27
22	13.91	9.66	14.41	–4.25	.50
23	34.30	32.11	34.17	–2.19	–.13
24	6.14	6.55	6.47	.41	.33
25	103.12	102.52	102.67	–.60	–.45
26	52.09	52.33	51.85	.24	–.24
27	48.54	48.89	48.58	.35	.04
28	97.04	97.86	96.24	.82	–.80
29	23.52	19.73	25.42	–3.79	1.90
30	16.60	17.22	16.40	.62	–.20
31	—	8.78	8.76	—	—
32	—	43.24	41.57	—	—
33	21.02	22.23	21.45	1.21	.43
34	1.12	1.25	1.29	.13	.17
35	—	2.74	2.20	—	—
36	10.51	9.78	10.98	–.73	.47
37	42.74	43.37	43.27	.63	.53
38	49.00	49.30	49.38	.30	.38
39	57.70	58.49	58.09	.79	.39

$$\sum_{i=1}^{33} (X'_i - \bar{X}_i)^2 = 65.4998 \qquad \sum_{i=1}^{33} (X''_i - \bar{X}_i)^2 = 14.4291$$

*Table 5–1, p. 81, lists the sectors both by number and descriptions.
Source: Calculated by author from figures provided by Central Statistical Office of Finland.

for the above-described transformation in approximating from a given base year's structure the structure of a year different from the base year.

Although by this measure the adjusted matrix fits the observations better than the 1956 matrix, it is natural to ask how significant the improvement is. A simple test will therefore be made to find out how likely it is that an apparent improvement of this magnitude could have taken place if some "random" adjustment of the 1956 matrix had been made. (In the extreme case we might have altered each input-output coefficient by adding to it some random number.) An arbitrary adjustment might be expected to improve estimates of some outputs and to make others worse. What is the probability that output levels based on the transformed matrix more closely approximate the calculated or observed 1952 output levels than output levels based on the untransformed matrix; that is, what is the probability that $|X''_i - \overline{X}_i|$ $(i = 1, 2, \ldots, 39)$ is smaller than $|X'_i - \overline{X}_i|$ $(i = 1, 2, \ldots, 39)$?

Imagine adding random numbers to the 1956 Finnish input-output coefficients. Each time we add a set of such numbers we obtain a new matrix with a corresponding pair of price and output vectors. Such vectors are sets of random variables. We do not know, of course, how these variables might be distributed, and therefore must approach them from a distribution-free (nonparametric) point of view. There is a nonparametric statistical test (the Sign Test) in which the only underlying assumption is that the variable under consideration form a continuous distribution. Essentially the nonparametric method to be applied is a test for the null hypothesis that two populations have the same location, and is designed for an analysis in which the same size sample is taken from each of the populations and in which the sample values are paired. We take each vector to be a sample and each calculated output to be an observation in the sample. We then assume that by altering the input-output coefficients we can derive continuous distributions of outputs.

Let $f_1\ (x_1)$ and $f_2(x_2)$ be two continuous frequency functions under consideration and let (x_{11}, x_{21}), (x_{12}, x_{22}), . . . , (x_{1n}, x_{2n}) denote n paired sample values to be drawn from the two populations. Consider the hypothesis

$$H_o : f_1(x_1) = f_2(x_2) \tag{73}$$

For purposes of testing this hypothesis it is convenient to consider the following differences: $x_{1i} - x_{2i}$ $(i = 1, 2, \ldots, n)$.

> Since the probability that the first of 2 sample values will exceed the second is the same as the probability that the second will exceed the first, and since, theoretically, the probability of a tie is 0, it follows that the probability that $x_{1i} - x_{2i}$ will be positive is $\frac{1}{2}$.[8]

Define

$$Z_i = \begin{cases} 1, \text{ if } (x_{1i} - x_{2i}) > 0 \\ 0, \text{ if } (x_{1i} - x_{2i}) < 0 \end{cases} \tag{74}$$

than Z_i is a variable corresponding to a single trial of an "event for which $P = \frac{1}{2}$." If the Z_is are independent, their sum

$$Z = \sum_{i=1}^{n} Z_i \tag{75}$$

is a variable corresponding to n independent trials of an "event for which $P = \frac{1}{2}$."[9]

In order to test H_o, consider as an alternative to H_o the hypothesis

$$H_1 : f_1(x_1) = f_2(x_2 + k) \tag{76}$$

where k is a positive constant. Under H_1, the x_{1i}s will tend to be larger than the x_{2i}s and Z will tend to exceed its expected value, $n/2$. Thus the appropriate critical region will be the right tail of the binomial distribution. If k had been negative, implying a tendency for $x_{1i} < x_{2i}$ and for Z to be less

---

[8] Paul G. Hoel, *Introduction to Mathematical Statistics* (2d ed.; New York: John Wiley and Sons, Inc., 1954), p. 285.

[9] *Ibid.*, p. 286.

than its expected value, the left tail of the binomial distribution would have been the appropriate rejection region.[10]

In applying this method to the problem of determining whether the transformed structure more closely approximates the true 1952 structure than does the structure of the base year—assuming no change in the technical parameters—we are interested in whether the absolute errors are less. Let x_{1i} $(i = 1, 2, \ldots, 39)$ represent the absolute difference between observed 1952 output and output based on the transformed matrix.

$$|X_i'' - \overline{X}_i| = x_{2i} \qquad (i = 1, 2, \ldots, 39) \tag{77}$$

and x_{2i} $(i = 1, 2, \ldots, 39)$ represent the absolute difference between observed 1952 output and output based on the original or untransformed matrix

$$|X_i' - \overline{X}_i| = x_{2i} \qquad (i = 1, 2, \ldots, 39) \tag{78}$$

If the differences $(x_{1i} - x_{2i})$ are negative, estimates based on the transformed matrix are more accurate than those based on the untransformed matrix. If, however, such differences are positive the reverse relationship holds. For all industries, Table 5–2 shows 10 positive and 21 negative differences (two ties occurred which are excluded from the analysis and the six sectors for which adequate data are lacking are also excluded); hence, $Z = 10$. Since for samples of this size the normal approximation of the binomial distribution can be used, Z may be treated as approximately normal.

It is expected that $x_{1i} < x_{2i}$, therefore the null hypothesis is

$$H_o : f_1(x_1) = f_2(x_2) \tag{79}$$

with its alternative as

$$H_1 : f_1(x_1) = f_2(x_2 - k) \tag{80}$$

---

[10]The above description of the Sign Test was taken from the following sources: P. G. Hoel, *op. cit.*, pp. 285–88; K. A. Brownlee, *Statistical Theory and Methodology in Science and Engineering* (New York: John Wiley and Sons, Inc., 1960), pp. 180–84; B. W. Lindgren, *Statistical Theory* (New York: The Macmillan Company, 1962), pp. 348–50; Sidney Siegel, *Nonparametric Statistics for the Behavioral Sciences* (New York: McGraw-Hill Book Co., 1956), pp. 68–75.

The left tail of the Z distribution will be the appropriate critical region. Therefore

$$\tau = \frac{10.5 - 15.5}{\frac{1}{2}\sqrt{31}} = -1.80$$

hence the probability that $Z \leq 10.5$ is .03513 and the null hypothesis is rejected at a .04 level of significance. That is to say, it is unlikely that we would have obtained as great an improvement in our estimates of Finnish output for 1952 had our alterations in the input-output matrix been governed by chance.

Thus on the basis of available evidence we conclude that for the Finnish economy over the period considered, the transformation (66)—which is based on the hypothesis that structural change is reflected in the corresponding price structure and the somewhat arbitrary choice of D as a diagonal matrix—compensates for at least certain of the structural changes which occurred between 1952 and 1956. The resulting technical matrix then in a sense does more closely approximate the true 1952 structure than does the technical matrix of the base year, 1956.

With empirical verification of the theoretical framework discussed earlier we are in a position to consider the Finnish indemnity within such a framework and to determine the real cost involved in effecting payments or deliveries.

6

INTERINDUSTRY ANALYSIS OF INDEMNITY PAYMENTS

With a basic description of the Finnish indemnity of 1944 (Chapter 1) and empirical verification (Chapter 5) of an appropriate input-output technique, we turn to a consideration of the impact of the indemnity on the various industries which comprise the Finnish economy.

The following shows, by use of the transformed input-output structure (transformed a_{ij}s), the interindustry relations that existed during the period of indemnity payments, the real cost—levels of gross production—associated with effecting such payments, plus the implications of the indemnity when considered in terms of constant or 1952 marks. Although evidence presented verifies that the transformed matrix more closely approximates the true structure of the final indemnity year than does the 1956 matrix, it is natural to ask how results based on the 1956 matrix differ from those based on the transformed matrix. We will, therefore, consider, first, the effects of the indemnity payments made in 1952 only; second, the implications of the payments expressed in 1952 marks; third, the effects and associated real cost—levels of gross production—of the total indemnity bill; and fourth, the differences in results based on the transformed and the untransformed matrices; that is, the effects of failure to correct for certain shifted input patterns. (Since it is impossible to estimate directly the 1952 a_{ij}s, it is necessary to employ the transformed a_{ij}s which approximate the unknown 1952 a_{ij}s.)

Effects of 1952 Reparation Payments

The input-output technique previously described permits us to determine for each industry or sector contained within the Finnish system a quantitative measure of the reparation's impact. That is, given the technological structure embodied in the transformed a_{ij}s and two outside bills of goods—one which includes payments under the indemnity account, Y'_i, and one from which such payments have been eliminated, Y''_i—a set of output levels corresponding to each of the outside bills of goods can be derived as follows:

$$X' = (I - A\ (\text{tranf}))^{-1} Y' \qquad (81)$$

$$X'' = (I - A\ (\text{tranf}))^{-1} Y'' \qquad (82)$$

The difference between the corresponding output levels, $X'_i - X''_i$ $(i = 1, 2, \ldots, 39)$, represents the effect of the indemnity payment on each of the individual sectors.

Table 6–1 lists by sectors all 1952 payments made to the Soviet Union under reparations along with output levels, X'_i and X''_i $(i = 1, 2, \ldots, 39)$, their corresponding differences, $X'_i - X''_i$ $(i = 1, 2, \ldots, 39)$, and the percent of output absorbed by such payments, $(X'_i - X''_i / X'_i$ $(i = 1, 2, \ldots, 39)$. The total bill paid in 1952 amounted to some 8.215 billion marks (calculated in 1952 marks). That is, during the final indemnity years the Finns delivered to the Soviet Union reparations, principally transport equipment and machinery, including electrical machinery, valued at 8.215 billion marks.

Reference to columns (4) and (5), Table 6–1, indicates that although reparation commodities per se were produced in only five of the sectors, a certain amount of output from all but seven sectors was required as necessary requisites in effecting delivery of the specified items. No deliveries, for example, were made directly from the basic metal sector—smelting and refining—but some 4.85 percent of calculated output from that sector was required in the manufacture of those items which were included. About 1.9 percent of output from the mining and quarrying sector was likewise required.

In the case of electrical machinery, appliances, and so forth, 1.4 billion marks in output was needed to effect payments of less than half that amount (.566 billion marks). For manufactured transport equipment, on the other hand, 6.31 billion marks in output was a required requisite for effecting payment—mainly in ships—of an almost equal amount, 6.166 billion marks.

Considered in terms of production, both direct and indirect, we find that while reparations per se in 1952 amounted to 8.215 billion marks, the total cost—gross production—associated with effecting these payments amounted to some 14.67 billion marks. That is, the total cost or level of production involved in effecting the 1952 payments was a little less than twice the actual bill. The important point, however, is that this represents less than 1 percent (.98) of total 1952 output and emphasizes the fact that by the concluding year of payments the effects of reparations had been reduced to a minimum.

Furthermore, apart from those industries which produced reparations directly, substantially less than 1 percent of each sector's current output was required in effecting the 1952 payments. (In the case of the basic metals and mining and quarrying output more than 1 percent of the current levels—4.85 and 1.96, respectively—was required.) For those sectors or industries from which payments were made directly, it is expected that a much larger proportion of their output levels would have been absorbed by reparations, but even here the percent of current output required from each sector in effecting the payments is impressively small; .88 percent of nonmetallic mineral products, 2.23 percent of metal products except machinery and transport equipment, 8.35 percent of machinery, 9.72 percent of electrical machinery, appliances, and so forth, and 18.51 percent of transport equipment.

TABLE 6–1

Impact of 1952 Reparation Payments on 39 Sectors Comprising the Finnish Economy

(Billions of 1952 Marks)

Sector	(1) 1952 Reparation Deliveries	(2) X'_i	(3) X''_i	(4) $(X'_i - X''_i)$	(5)* $(X'_i - X''_i)/X'_i$
1. Agriculture		187.01	186.98	.03	.016
2. Hunting and fishing		3.23	3.23	.00	.000
3. Forestry		89.77	89.63	.14	.156
4. Mining and quarrying		6.23	6.11	.12	1.960
5. Food manufacturing industries		151.57	151.56	.01	.007
6. Beverage industries		7.22	7.22	.00	.000
7. Tobacco manufactures		4.85	4.85	.00	.000
8. Manufacture of textiles		44.73	44.71	.02	.045
9. Manufacture of footwear, other wearing apparel, and made-up textile goods		41.38	41.38	.00	.000
10. Manufacture of wood and cork, except manufacture of furniture		68.88	68.75	.13	.189
11. Manufacture of furniture and fixtures		12.95	12.92	.03	.023
12. Manufacture of paper and paper products		92.79	92.67	.12	.129
13. Printing, publishing, and allied industries		23.65	23.59	.06	.253
14. Manufacture of leather and leather products, except footwear		5.27	5.26	.01	.190
15. Manufacture of rubber products		7.10	7.07	.03	.425
16. Manufacture of chemicals and chemical products		27.37	27.18	.19	.695
17. Manufacture of products of petroleum and asphalt		1.64	1.63	.01	.610
18. Manufacture of nonmetallic mineral products	.0121	18.25	18.09	.16	.877
19. Basic metal industries		26.59	25.30	1.29	4.850
20. Manufacture of metal products, except machinery and transport equipment	.0258	18.36	17.95	.41	2.225

TABLE 6-1—*Continued*

Sector	(1) 1952 Reparation Deliveries	(2) X'_i	(3) X''_i	(4) $(X'_i - X''_i)$	(5)* $(X'_i - X''_i)/X'_i$
21. Manufacture of machinery, except electrical machinery	1.4445	35.99	32.98	3.01	8.352
22. Manufacture of electrical machinery, apparatus, appliances, and supplies	.5665	14.41	13.01	1.40	9.720
23. Manufacture of transport equipment	6.1664	34.17	27.86	6.31	18.510
24. Miscellaneous industries		6.47	6.46	.01	.154
25. House construction		102.67	102.59	.08	.077
26. Other construction		51.85	51.82	.03	.058
27. Electricity, gas, steam, and water services		48.58	48.24	.34	.405
28. Trade		96.24	96.14	.10	.010
29. Banking and insurance		25.42	25.30	.12	.473
30. Railway transport		16.40	16.32	.08	.485
31. Tramway and bus transport		8.76	8.76	.00	.000
32. Other road transport		41.57	41.41	.16	.384
33. Water transport		21.45	21.31	.14	.186
34. Air transport		1.29	1.29	.00	.000
35. Services incidental to transport		2.20	2.18	.02	.909
36. Communication		10.98	10.92	.06	.545
37. Central government		43.27	43.26	.01	.023
38. Local authorities		49.38	49.38	.00	.000
39. Other services		58.01	58.05	.04	.069
Total	8.2153	1,507.95		14.67	

*Figures in column (5) are percents—decimal has been moved two places to the right.
SOURCE: Calculated by author from figures provided by Central Statistical Office of Finland.

Thus we can say that the 1952 payments were not the arduous bill that one might have suspected. Contrary to conjecture, payments made during the final year were well within the range of economic possibility. Nearly three-fourths of the 1952 bill came from manufactured transport equipment; this, however, represented only 18.4 percent of that sector's output. The remaining quarter came primarily from manufactured machinery, including electrical machinery, and absorbed less than 9 percent of output in those sectors. Thus, in terms of Finland's capacity to effect payments, had the Soviet Union placed greater emphasis on deliveries in the latter as opposed to the earlier years, they would have been able to exact a bill far in excess of the one actually paid and still have been within Finland's production possibility schedules.

Recall that during the final stage of reparations the incident of the indemnity shifted from the wood to the metal-working industries, principally to the shipbuilding and allied industries. The result of the shifted emphasis was that deliveries of certain kinds of new vessels and related products were in arrears through most of the final payment period. Available evidence indicates, however, that the basic problem was not the extremely arduous bill generally purported, but rather a capacity restraint in certain of the shipbuilding industries along with the inability to acquire, either domestically or from abroad, needed requisite materials.

Evaluation of Reparations in 1952 Marks

If we evaluate both the annual payments and the total bill in terms of 1952 marks, for example, we are in effect calculating a volume index of payments. Such an index (Table 6–2) shows that in terms of goods delivered nearly 21 percent of the entire bill was paid in 1945. After 1950, however, annual payments accounted for less than 6 percent of the total bill. In other words, in real terms annual payments were progressively reduced.

Considered from the Finnish point of view the burden of payments was greatest at a time when the economy was least able to meet the demands and was reduced only after a suitable industrial structure with sufficient capacity had been created. That is, if the annual payments had been progressively increased instead of decreased the burden of effecting the payments would have been substantially less. We have already seen that by 1952 the impact of payments had been reduced to a minimum requiring less than 1 percent of total output. On the other hand it is quite reasonable to assume that in the immediate postwar years, before needed expansion had been realized, annual payments represented a much larger proportion of total output.

Considered from the Russian point of view, had the annual payments been progressively increased instead of decreased they could have bettered their position. That is, they could have exacted a bill representing compensation for war damage inflicted upon them far in excess of the bill which was actually paid. According to the original schedule annual payments were to equal $50 million each. At the end of the first indemnity year it was obvious that such payments far exceeded the capacity of certain key industries. The Soviets, therefore, extended the period of payments from six to eight years, which in terms of the original agreement meant annual payments of $35.5 million. Again in 1948 the burden was lightened when half of the outstanding deliveries was cancelled. Had the Soviets placed the emphasis on the latter as opposed to the earlier deliveries, they would not, at least on economic grounds, have been compelled to grant these reductions in payments. In fact, evidence indicates that by progressively increasing the annual payments they could have exacted a bill in excess of the original $300 million without serious impact on the Finnish economy; that is, without exceeding production possibility schedules. Thus we see that had payments been progressively increased instead of decreased it would have been advantageous to both the debtor and the creditor.

TABLE 6–2

FINNISH REPARATION PAYMENTS BY YEARS AND SECTORS

(Millions of 1952 Marks) *

Sector	1944	1945	1946	1947	1948
Mining and quarrying		1.2			
Manufacture of textiles		.5	.1		2.4
Manufacture of footwear, other wearing apparel, and made-up textile goods			1.1		
Manufacture of wood and cork, except manufacture of furniture	907.4	8,481.8	4,344.7	2,812.1	1,594.7
Manufacture of paper and paper products	1,099.2	13,785.3	5,232.2	3,881.7	2,227.6
Printing, publishing, and allied industries		1.0		.5	3.8
Manufacture of leather and leather products			.1		
Manufacture of rubber products					.1
Manufacture of chemicals and chemical products			1.5	2.9	.8
Manufacture of nonmetallic mineral products		2.4	233.9	48.0	47.9
Basic metal industries		21.4	874.4	61.6	145.3
Manufacture of metal products, except machinery and transport equipment	37.1	1,439.3	420.3	1,733.2	1,187.7
Manufacture of machinery, except electrical machinery		1,706.3	7,719.9	5,004.5	5,477.3
Manufacture of electrical machinery, apparatus, appliances, and supplies		1,480.8	542.1	2,548.0	1,963.4
Manufacture of transport equipment		9,352.9	6,354.9	8,571.6	9,024.3
Miscellaneous industries					.3
Total	2,043.7	36,271.9	25,725.2	24,664.1	21,675.6

TABLE 6-2—*Continued*

Sector	1949	1950	1951	1952	Total
Mining and quarrying					1.2
Manufacture of textiles	.4				3.4
Manufacture of footwear, other wearing apparel, and made-up textile goods					1.1
Manufacture of wood and cork, except manufacture of furniture	50.3				18,191.0
Manufacture of paper and paper products	77.4				26,303.4
Printing, publishing, and allied industries					5.3
Manufacture of leather and leather products		.1			.2
Manufacture of rubber products	.4	.3			.8
Manufacture of chemicals and chemical products	3.3				8.5
Manufacture of nonmetallic mineral products	81.9	26.6	10.7	12.1	463.5
Basic metal industries	289.2	28.0			1,419.9
Manufacture of metal products, except machinery and transport equipment	775.5	57.6	66.4	25.8	5,742.9
Manufacture of machinery, except electrical machinery	7,358.7	2,292.5	2,163.0	1,444.5	33,166.7
Manufacture of electrical machinery, apparatus, appliances, and supplies	2,602.5	1,267.4	897.3	566.5	11,868.0
Manufacture of transport equipment	10,681.8	6,523.9	10,498.5	6,166.4	67,174.3
Miscellaneous industries	22.7	5.0	.1		28.1
Total	21,944.1	10,201.4	13,636.0	8,215.3	164,378.3

*Annual payments by sectors have been expressed in 1952 marks by use of price deflators corresponding to the following industries: timber, pulp and paper, spinning and weaving, leather and rubber, basic metal, manufacture of machinery, mineral, chemical and nonmetallic mineral except petroleum and coal. Where the appropriate price deflators were not available approximations were used which, by nature, introduces certain errors.

SOURCE: Calculated by author from figures provided by Central Statistical Office of Finland.

Effects of the Total Reparation Bill

As indicated in a previous discussion, an interindustry study of the Finnish economy during the indemnity period implies structural knowledge for each year of payments. Available data, however, apart from the reparations per se, permits a transformation of the base year's structure, the 1956 a_{ij}s, to represent the 1952 structure only. Inherent in this limitation is the assumption that all goods delivered to the Soviet Union under the indemnity account were produced with 1952 technology.

With this assumption, the total indemnity bill, calculated in 1952 marks (Table 6–2), can be used to replace the final or outside bill of goods in the transformed input-output equations. This permits us to derive a set of production levels which correspond to output requirements from each sector necessary in effecting the total payments.

The result of making the above substitutions and solving for the corresponding output levels (Table 6–3) indicates that the total cost—level of direct plus indirect production—associated with deliveries valued at 164,378.3 million marks —the total indemnity bill expressed in 1952 marks—amounted to some 286,025.3 million or 286.02 billion marks. That is, costs encountered by the Finns in discharging their obligation under the indemnity agreement totaled 164,378.3 million marks of direct production—goods transferred directly—plus another 121,647.0 million marks of indirect production—goods which were not included in the payments per se, but which were necessary in effecting the transfer of those which were included.

While the indemnity per se was produced basically in 8 of the sectors, output from 37 of the 39 sectors was required in effecting the transfer. In other words, for the indemnity account, all but two of the sectors—hunting and fishing and tobacco manufacture—were involved in indirect production —supporting or intermediate inputs—while only 8 of the sectors were involved in direct production. (Technically speaking, 16 sectors produced reparations directly, but for 8 of these such production was minimal and of no particular consequence.)

The assumption that the entire indemnity bill was produced with technology as defined by the transformed input-output structure implies that production costs are somewhat understated. Changes within the technical structure between 1944 and 1952 conceivably created, at least for certain of the sectors, more efficient input-output parameters. It is this more efficient set of parameters that is approximated by the transformed a_{ij}s and consequently computations based on them will in general somewhat understate the effects of the indemnity bill on the corresponding output levels.

The Effects of Reparations Based on Both the Transformed and Untransformed Matrices

While available evidence verifies the transformed matrix as a better approximation of the 1952 structure than the untransformed or base year matrix, it is natural to ask how results of the analysis would have been altered had no adjustments been made to compensate for shifted input patterns. That is, were output levels based on both the transformed and the untransformed matrices with the autonomous or outside bill of goods replaced by the indemnity bill sufficiently different to justify using the transformed input-output coefficients?

An approach to the problem is presented in Table 6–4, where the transformed and the untransformed matrices have been combined with the total indemnity bill to derive output levels as follows:

$$(I - A\text{ (tranf) })^{-1}R = X_r' \qquad (83)$$

$$(I - A(56)\ )^{-1}R = X_r'' \qquad (84)$$

where R represents the total indemnity bill expressed in 1952 marks.

Accordingly, the total cost of the indemnity (direct plus

TABLE 6–3

Impact of Total Reparation Payments on 39 Sectors Comprising the Finnish Economy

(Billions of 1952 Marks)

Sector	(1)* Total Reparation Deliveries	(2)† Calculated 1952 Output Levels (X'_i)	(3)‡ Outputs Required to Effect Total Payments (X'_{ri})	(4)§ X'_i/X'_{ri}
1. Agriculture		187.01	2.31	1.24
2. Hunting and fishing		3.23	.00	.00
3. Forestry		89.77	18.67	20.80
4. Mining and quarrying	.0012	6.23	2.21	35.47
5. Food manufacturing industries		151.57	.21	.14
6. Beverage industries		7.22	.02	.28
7. Tobacco manufactures		4.85	.00	.00
8. Manufacture of textiles	.0034	44.73	.35	.78
9. Manufacture of footwear, other wearing apparel, and made-up textile goods	.0011	41.38	.01	.02
10. Manufacture of wood and cork, except manufacture of furniture	18.1910	68.88	22.28	32.35
11. Manufacture of furniture and fixtures		12.95	.48	3.71
12. Manufacture of paper and paper products	26.3034	92.79	38.29	41.26
13. Printing, publishing, and allied industries	.0053	23.65	1.06	4.48
14. Manufacture of leather and leather products, except footwear	.0002	5.27	.15	2.85
15. Manufacture of rubber products	.0008	7.10	.45	6.34
16. Manufacture of chemical and chemical products	.0085	27.37	3.98	14.54
17. Manufacture of products of petroleum and asphalt		1.64	.11	6.71
18. Manufacture of nonmetallic mineral products	.4635	18.25	1.14	6.25
19. Basic metal industries	1.4199	26.59	20.89	78.56
20. Manufacture of metal products, except machinery and transport equipment	5.7429	18.36	10.98	59.80

TABLE 6–3—*Continued*

Sector	(1)* Total Reparation Deliveries	(2)† Calculated 1952 Output Levels (X'_i)	(3)‡ Outputs Required to Effect Total Payments (X'_{ri})	(4)§ X'_i/X'_{ri}
21. Manufacture of machinery, except electrical machinery	33.1667	35.99	40.55	112.67
22. Manufacture of electrical machinery, apparatus, appliances, and supplies	11.8680	14.41	22.44	155.73
23. Manufacture of transport equipment	67.1743	34.17	69.25	202.66
24. Miscellaneous industries	.0281	6.47	.14	2.16
25. House construction		102.67	1.64	1.60
26. Other construction		51.85	.49	.94
27. Electricity, gas, steam, and water services		48.58	12.86	26.47
28. Trade		96.24	1.75	1.82
29. Banking and insurance		25.42	3.41	13.41
30. Railway transport		16.40	1.68	10.24
31. Tramway and bus transport		8.76	.04	.46
32. Other road transport		41.57	3.92	9.43
33. Water transport		21.45	2.11	9.84
34. Air transport		1.29	.03	2.32
35. Services incidental to transport		2.20	.20	9.09
36. Communication		10.98	.96	8.74
37. Central government		43.27	.18	.42
38. Local authorities		49.38	.05	.10
39. Other services		58.01	.72	1.24
Totals	164.3783	1,507.95	286.02	18.97

*See Table 6–2, page 101.
†See Table 6–1, page 96.
‡See Table 6–4, page 106.
§The decimal has been moved two places to the right so that the numbers appear as percents.
SOURCE: Calculated by author from figures provided by Central Statistical Office of Finland.

TABLE 6–4

A COMPARISON OF OUTPUTS REQUIRED BY INDEMNITY PAYMENTS AS BASED ON BOTH THE TRANSFORMED AND UNTRANSFORMED MATRICES

(Millions of 1952 Marks)

Sector	(1)* X'_{ri}	(2)† X''_{ri}	(3) $(X'_{ri} - X''_{ri})$	(4)‡ $(X'_{ri} - X''_{ri})/X'_{ri}$
1. Agriculture	2,311.20	2,132.46	178.74	7.73
2. Hunting and fishing	.00	.00	.00	.00
3. Forestry	18,674.43	19,402.01	–727.58	3.90
4. Mining and quarrying	2,214.06	2,122.89	91.17	4.12
5. Food manufacturing industries	212.31	196.89	15.42	7.26
6. Beverage industries	17.48	10.75	6.73	38.50
7. Tobacco manufactures	.00	.00	.00	.00
8. Manufacture of textiles	348.74	492.94	–144.20	41.35
9. Manufacture of footwear, other wearing apparel, and made-up textile goods	8.59	1.15	7.44	86.61
10. Manufacture of wood and cork, except manufacture of furniture	22,283.29	22,508.84	–225.55	1.01
11. Manufacture of furniture and fixtures	478.56	374.97	103.59	21.65
12. Manufacture of paper and paper products	38,290.81	38,549.57	–258.76	.68
13. Printing, publishing, and allied industries	1,065.83	1,298.23	–232.40	21.80
14. Manufacture of leather and leather products, except footwear	149.50	182.29	–32.79	21.93
15. Manufacture of rubber products	451.11	483.89	–32.78	7.27
16. Manufacture of chemicals and chemical products	3,980.77	4,906.02	–925.25	23.24
17. Manufacture of products of petroleum and asphalt	105.79	121.88	–16.09	15.21
18. Manufacture of nonmetallic mineral products	1,136.49	1,211.11	–74.62	6.56
19. Basic metal industries	20,893.01	23,729.21	–2,836.20	13.57
20. Manufacture of metal products, except machinery and transport equipment	10,982.78	11,725.80	–743.02	6.76

TABLE 6-4—*Continued*

Sector	(1)* X'_{ri}	(2)† X''_{ri}	(3) $(X'_{ri} - X''_{ri})$	(4)‡ $(X'_{ri} - X''_{ri})/X'_{r_i}$
21. Manufacture of machinery, except electrical machinery	40,547.18	41,683.76	−1,136.58	2.80
22. Manufacture of electrical machinery, apparatus, appliances, and supplies	22,435.83	19,246.55	3,189.28	14.22
23. Manufacture of transport equipment	69,248.06	69,153.17	94.89	.14
24. Miscellaneous industries	137.98	152.59	−14.61	10.59
25. House construction	1,641.88	1,674.03	−32.15	1.59
26. Other construction	485.68	747.26	−261.58	53.86
27. Electricity, gas, steam, and water services	12,856.89	12,751.75	105.14	.82
28. Trade	1,754.67	1,949.08	−194.41	11.08
29. Banking and insurance	3,414.68	2,685.88	728.80	21.34
30. Railway transport	1,683.09	1,937.71	−254.62	15.13
31. Tramway and bus transport	44.18	45.22	−1.04	2.35
32. Other road transport	3,923.42	4,238.97	−315.55	8.04
33. Water transport	2,111.39	2,609.28	−497.89	23.58
34. Air transport	26.70	16.59	10.11	37.86
35. Services incidental to transport	202.88	228.06	−25.18	12.41
36. Communication	957.47	880.03	77.44	8.09
37. Central government	181.97	200.40	−18.43	10.13
38. Local authorities	46.06	38.33	7.73	16.78
39. Other services	720.55	794.42	−73.87	10.25
Totals	286,025.31	290,483.98	13,691.63§	

*$(I - A\ (\text{tranf}))^{-1}R = X'_r$, where R is the total reparations bill calculated in 1952 marks.
†$(I - A(56))^{-1}R = X''_r$, where R is the total reparations bill calculated in 1952 marks.
‡The decimal has been moved two places to the right so that numbers appear as percents.
§Sum of absolute differences.
SOURCE: Calculated by author from figures provided by Central Statistical Office of Finland.

indirect production) projected on the basis of the transformed structure is found to represent a slightly smaller total bill (286,025.3 million marks) than that projected on the basis of the untransformed structure (290,483.98 million marks). The two costs or production estimates, however, differ only by 1.56 percent, which would indicate that the effects of the transformation were nominal and of no particular consequence.

If, on the other hand, we consider the differences $(X'_{ri} - X''_{ri})$ $(i = 1, 2, \ldots, 39)$, it is recognized that offsetting or counterbalancing errors tend to minimize the effect of the transformation as reflected in the aggregate figures. That is, the positive errors, $X'_{ri} > X''_{ri}$, are offset by negative errors, $X'_{ri} < X''_{ri}$, with only the difference of their sums appearing in the estimated totals.

Furthermore, column (4) of Table 6-4 shows that production levels based on the original untransformed coefficients deviate from those based on the transformed coefficients by more than 20 percent in 11 of the sectors and by more than 10 percent in 21 of the sectors. Thus, considered on a disaggregated—individual sector—basis, we see that the effects of the transformation were more extensive than perhaps is implied by consideration of aggregate, or total, costs only.

It was stated previously that the total cost of the indemnity as derived on the basis of the transformed structure represented a minimum cost which somewhat understated the true cost. By similar reasoning one would expect the a_{ij}s derived from 1956 observations to understate such costs even further. Since, however, the 1956 a_{ij}s project the largest bill —total cost—for certain of the sectors or industries the 1952 input-output parameters must be considered more efficient than corresponding 1956 parameters. It must be pointed out, however, that for a given final bill of goods $X''_{ri} > X'_{ri}$ is not sufficient to guarantee that the *i*th sector per se has become less efficient, or $X''_{ri} < X'_{ri}$ to guarantee that it has become more efficient. The former condition could result from sector *j* requiring more of *i*'s output; that is, $a''_{ij} > a'_{ij}$, the later from

$a''_{ij} < a'_{ij}$ while the coefficients of the ith sector remains unchanged.

In order to meet the indemnity demands the Finns were compelled to expand greatly their existing capacity and in certain cases to create entirely new industries. As a result of indemnity pressures and heavy price controls, especially in the reparation industries, much of the increased capacity was extremely inefficient. Hence, with the relaxing of price controls in the early '50s and particularly after the payments were completed, in 1952, prices rose substantially. According to the basic hypothesis of the proposed transformation, namely that changes in the input-output coefficients are reflected in the price structure, we would expect to see alterations in the coefficients of those industries for which prices rose. This may in part explain why certain industries were less efficient in 1956 than in 1952.

Summary

The above considerations add up to the conclusion that even though the Finns encountered certain difficulties in meeting their obligation, their basic problem was not the timetable or the bill of goods specified by the indemnity recipients. With regard to effecting delivery of the specified bill one might say that the Finns managed rather well. The real problem, it appears, was one of capacity restraints in certain of the key industries, primarily in the shipbuilding industry, and the inability to acquire either from domestic or foreign sources certain raw and semimanufactured materials. On the whole, evidence suggests that the indemnity burden was not as extensive as one might perhaps suspect.

Considered in terms of the 1952 payments only, three-fourths of the bill came from manufactured transport equipment—mainly ships—but absorbed only 18.4 percent of that sector's current output. Unfortunately, available data does not permit a similar analysis for years prior to 1952. Since, however, the basic structure of the bill did not change after 1948—manufactured transport equipment and machines, including electrical machines—it is unlikely that the problems encountered in these years were substantially different from those encountered in 1952.

Between 1944 and 1948 the weight of the indemnity was balanced between the wood and metalworking industries. The former of these, traditionally Finland's staple export industry, required certain renovations immediately following the war but encountered no serious problems, capacity or otherwise, in meeting its share of the indemnity. The metal industries, on the other hand, were greatly expanded in the immediate postwar years. By 1952, however, payments absorbed only a fraction of current production in these areas, indicating a capacity increase far in excess of what was required by reparations.

Apart from annual installments, the total bill, considered in terms of both direct and indirect production needed to effect the transfer, does not appear to have been outside the range of economic possibility. If, for example, the entire bill had been paid out of 1952 production only, 78.56 percent of output from the basic metals, 59.80 percent from manufacture of metal products, along with 41.26 percent of output from the manufacture of wood and 32.35 percent from the manufacture of paper, would have been absorbed. Indirectly 20.8 and 35.5 percent of output from forestry and mining, respectively, would have been required. In the case of transport equipment, machinery, including electrical machinery, and so on, 1952 production would not have been sufficient to meet demands. In spite of this, however, there is little evidence to indicate that reparations posed for the Finns a bill which pushed production possibility schedules to the limit.

In this regard, it is quite clear that had the Soviet Union in the basic agreement specified that annual payments be progressively increased instead of decreased, it would have been mutually advantageous. For the Finns the major impact of the burden would have come at a point when the industrial structure was ready to meet the demands. On the other hand the Soviets could have exacted a larger bill without encountering the problem of capacity restraints.

Considered strictly from a production point of view, reparations do not appear to have been overly burdensome. From an unfavorable trade balance point of view, however, it might well be argued that reparations did create serious problems. For most of the payment period the Finnish trade balance was seriously out of adjustment; that is, imports greatly exceeded exports. Clearly imports were increased as a result of reparations—importation of raw and semimanufactured materials needed to effect the indemnity transfer. On the other hand, commodities which normally would have appeared on the commercial export market were absorbed by reparations, thus tending to worsen still further the trade balance. In this sense, there is a valid argument that reparations did pose for the Finns rather formidable problems.

Furthermore, the transformation of input-output parameters suggests that for certain industries, the 1956 coefficients were less efficient than the corresponding 1952 coefficients. This can, in part, be explained by the natural inefficiencies created by the reparations plus the heavy price controls which were relaxed only after the payments were nearly completed. Since the transformed matrix more nearly represents the 1952 structure, and thus accounts for such efficiency changes, we employ it in analyzing the indemnity payments. Even in its present imperfect form such a transformation represents an approach to the analysis of an industrial structure for which it is impossible to calculate directly the relevant a_{ij}s.

Appendixes

A

CHANGES IN TECHNICAL COEFFICIENTS

The study of structural change involves comparison of the technical coefficients of an input-output matrix at two points in time. If the coefficients are identical, the implication is that the structure of all sectors included remained invariant over the period considered. If, on the other hand, the coefficients are not identical, the implication is that the structure of at least certain of the sectors underwent change.

The simplest index of change of any one particular coefficient between two points in time is the difference between its final and its original value; that is, $a_{ij}(t) - a_{ij}(t + 1)$. Since the absolute magnitude of any one a_{ij} depends upon the physical units in which the inputs and outputs are described such a difference would be of little use for comparison of changes in two or more different coefficients. To avoid this inconvenience, Leontief suggests that the differences can, for purposes of quantitative comparison, be related to the mean of the original and the final value of the coefficients. That is, if $a_{ij}(t)$ and $a_{ij}(t + 1)$ are the two values of a particular coefficient which are to be compared, their difference is $a_{ij}(t) - a_{ij}(t + 1)$, their mean is $\frac{(a_{ij}(t) + a_{ij}(t + 1))}{2}$, and the index of relative change is

$$a'_{ij} = \frac{2(a_{ij}(t) - a_{ij}(t+1))}{(a_{ij}(t) + a_{ij}(t+1))} \qquad (1)$$

If structural change were measured by an unweighted distribution of such indices it would fail to take into account the fact that certain of the input ratios, a_{ij}s, correspond to large, others to small, industries. To eliminate this source of possible distortion Leontief suggests that each index of change, a'_{ij} $(i, j = 1, 2, \ldots, m)$ be weighted according to

$$\frac{(x_{ij}(t) + x_{ij}(t+1))}{2} \qquad (i, j = 1, 2, \ldots, m) \qquad (2)$$

A positive change means a reduction in the input requirements per unit of output. In this sense there has been an increase in productivity. A negative change means an increase in the input requirements per unit of output and can be described as a decrease in productivity.[1]

Within the transformed input-output framework, however, it is not necessary, indeed it is highly unlikely, that each a_{ij} derived through the transformation will exactly equal the a_{ij} which it approximates. That is, a_{ij} (tranf) $\neq \bar{a}_{ij}$ $(i, j = 1, 2, \ldots, m)$ where $\bar{a}_{ij}$ is the value of the unknown input ratio which actually prevailed in 1952.

Therefore, for any given economy the structural change implied by a particular transformation of the input-output matrix—such as that suggested in Chapter 4—cannot be analyzed in terms of the individual coefficients as suggested by Leontief. There is no direct correspondence between the a_{ij}s in the transformed and true technical matrices, so that the measurement of structural change requires the use of an index of aggregated coefficients.

Consider, therefore, the row and the column sums of the inverse of the coefficient matrix. (Since changes within the structure of a system are reflected in both the coefficient

[1]W. Leontief, *Studies in the Structure of the American Economy* (New York: Oxford University Press, 1946), pp. 23–75.

matrix and its inverse, we may for convenience approach the problem of structural change in terms of the inverse matrix only.)

If A_{ij}, an element of the inverse of the open matrix, is defined to be the increase in output of the ith industry necessary for a one unit increase in final demand of the jth industry's output, the sum

$$\sum_{i=1}^{m} A_{ij} \qquad (j = 1, 2, \ldots, m) \tag{3}$$

is the total increase in output from the whole system of industries necessary for a one unit increase in final demand for the jth industry's output. Considered at two different points in time the above sum may be compared as follows

$$\sum_{i=1}^{m} A_{ij}(t) \gtreqless \sum_{i=1}^{m} A_{ij}(t+1) \qquad (j = 1, 2, \ldots, m) \tag{4}$$

If the left term exceeds the right it implies that more output from all industries was needed at t than at $t + 1$ to effect a unit increase in final demand for the output of the jth industry. Similarly, if the right term exceeds the left, less output from all industries was needed at t than at $t + 1$ to effect a unit increase in final demand for the output of the jth industry. In a sense, the former condition can be described as an increase while the latter as a decrease in productivity. If the sums have been exactly equal, productivity, thus defined, would have remained constant.

On the other hand, the sum

$$\sum_{j=1}^{m} A_{ij} \qquad (i = 1, 2, \ldots, m) \tag{5}$$

is the increase in the ith industry's output necessary for a one unit increase in final demand for the output of each industry. Again, considered at two different points in time, we may make the comparison

$$\sum_{j=1}^{m} A_{ij}(t) \gtreqless \sum_{j=1}^{m} A_{ij}(t+1) \qquad (i = 1, 2, \ldots, m) \tag{6}$$

If the left term exceeds the right it implies that more of the

ith industry's output was required at t than at $t + 1$ to effect a unit increase in final demand for the output of each industry. Similarly, if the right term exceeds the left, less of the ith industry's output was required at t than at $t + 1$ to effect a unit increase in final demand for the output of each industry. Defined in this sense, the former situation represents an increase while the latter a decrease in productivity. It is important to recognize that we have defined productivity or efficiency in the two different ways—the increase in output from all industries needed to effect a unit increase in final demand for the output of one industry (column sums), and the increase of one industry's output needed to effect a unit increase in final demand for the output of each (all) industry (row sums).

Presented in these terms, it is possible to identify those sectors or industries for which productivity either increased, decreased, or remained constant. It is readily recognized, however, that although the incident of change is identifiable, the extent of change is left in question; that is, the efficiency of those sectors identified with change either increased or decreased, but the question of how much is left open.

While a complete description of such changes is not within the limits of the present framework, we can nevertheless indicate on a relative basis where productivity or efficiency changes were the greatest. Consider the following:

$$\sum_{i=1}^{m} \left(A_{ij}(t) - A_{ij}(t+1) \right) \gtreqless 0 \qquad (j = 1, 2, \ldots, m) \qquad (7)$$

If the efficiency of all industries producing for a unit increase in final demand of the jth industry's output increased (decreased) relative to that when producing for a unit increase in final demand for the kth industry's output, we can say that productivity increased (decreased) relatively more in the production of the jth output. (The sum of the jth columns in (7) will be positive and exceed that of the kth columns.) Further consider

$$\sum_{j=1}^{m} \left(A_{ij}(t) - A_{ij}(t+1) \right) \gtreqless 0 \qquad (i = 1, 2, \ldots, m) \qquad (8)$$

If the efficiency of the ith output as an input into the system —each industry—in effecting a unit increase in final demand for each industry's output increased (decreased) relative to that of the kth output, we can say that the productivity of the jth output increased (decreased) relative to that of the kth output. (The sum of the ith rows in (8) will be positive and exceed that of the kth rows.)

Therefore, on the basis of change implied by the transformed input-output matrix we can both identify the direction in which productivity changed—increased and decreased—and indicate in a relative sense where such changes were the greatest. Further, such a consideration implies that we can find a certain ranking of the various industries which lends itself to empirical verification. That is, on the basis of the transformed input-output matrix we can make certain predictions about how productivity changed which, in principle, can be tested empirically.

Thus efficiency or productivity changes give another method of checking the reliability of the particular transformation used. For the small economy of Finland, previous tests indicate that the transformed matrix is a better predictor of 1952 output than the 1956 matrix. If, however, additional evidence were to support our previous conclusions, we would be that much more justified in using the proposed transformation. (Since for the Finnish economy available data on productivity changes do not currently permit verification of the transformation in this way, we will consider only the major changes as indicated by the transformed matrix.)

For the Finnish economy the above calculations have been presented in Appendix Table A–1. Based on the inverses of the transformed and the original coefficient matrices these calculations indicate that efficiency of all 39 industries increased when producing to effect a unit increase in final demand for 24 of the outputs and decrease for the remaining 15 outputs. The greatest relative increases were for the outputs of printing and publishing, leather, and chemical products, while the greatest relative decreases were for the outputs of elec-

TABLE A–1

PRODUCTIVITY CHANGES OF THE FINNISH ECONOMY DEFINED IN TERMS OF THE APPROPRIATE INVERSE MATRICES

Row or Column*	Sums of Columns Tranf. Inv.	Sums of Columns '56 Inv.	Sums of Rows Tranf. Inv.	Sums of Rows '56 Inv.	Sums of Column Diff's	Sums of Row Diff's
1..........	2.021	2.048	3.260	3.194	−.027	+.066
2..........	1.058	1.064	1.005	1.004	−.006	+.001
3..........	1.174	1.154	2.761	2.968	+.020	−.207
4..........	1.656	1.739	1.570	1.509	−.083	+.061
5..........	2.506	2.535	1.743	1.698	−.029	+.045
6..........	2.082	2.053	1.238	1.238	+.029	000
7..........	1.800	1.739	1.017	1.017	+.061	000
8..........	1.432	1.369	1.601	1.672	+.063	−.071
9..........	1.782	1.747	1.045	1.048	+.035	−.003
10..........	1.948	1.943	1.780	1.906	+.005	−.126
11..........	1.525	1.869	1.140	1.103	−.344	+.037
12..........	2.284	2.274	2.899	2.853	+.010	+.046
13..........	2.095	1.752	1.904	1.651	+.343	+.253
14..........	1.773	1.648	1.163	1.165	+.125	−.002
15..........	1.375	1.491	1.158	1.153	−.116	+.005
16..........	1.721	1.630	2.088	2.282	+.091	−.194
17..........	1.695	1.636	1.055	1.055	+.059	000
18..........	1.600	1.719	1.533	1.540	−.119	−.007
19..........	2.516	2.483	3.197	3.373	+.033	−.176
20..........	1.633	1.614	1.512	1.562	+.019	−.050
21..........	1.698	1.644	1.475	1.522	+.054	−.047
22..........	1.533	1.819	1.690	1.470	−.286	+.220
23..........	1.522	1.571	2.319	2.122	+.049	+.197
24..........	1.490	1.484	1.073	1.075	+.006	−.002
25..........	1.722	1.723	1.618	1.609	−.001	+.009
26..........	1.770	1.792	1.503	1.502	−.022	+.001
27..........	2.088	2.085	3.488	3.645	+.003	−.157
28..........	1.368	1.349	1.782	1.822	+.019	−.040
29..........	1.112	1.149	1.962	1.743	−.037	+.219
30..........	1.744	1.846	1.569	1.610	−.102	−.041
31..........	1.523	1.487	1.044	1.050	+.036	−.006
32..........	1.399	1.364	2.158	2.319	+.035	−.161
33..........	1.246	1.200	1.423	1.466	+.046	−.043
34..........	1.639	1.570	1.019	1.017	+.069	+.002
35..........	1.386	1.376	1.056	1.057	+.010	−.001
36..........	1.353	1.384	1.356	1.309	−0.31	+.047
37..........	1.495	1.468	1.069	1.072	+0.27	−.003
38..........	1.495	1.605	1.007	1.005	−.110	+.002
39..........	1.449	1.419	1.426	1.437	+.030	−.011

*For a listing of sector titles corresponding to the row and column numbers refer to Table 5–1 page 81.

SOURCE: Inverse of the 1956 coefficient and the transformed matrices as presented in this study.

trical machinery, appliances, and so on, transport equipment, non-metallic mineral products, rubber products, and furniture. It was in certain of these areas—manufacture of machinery, including electrical machinery, appliances, and transport equipment—that capacity expansion was the most extensive; in some cases entirely new industries were created. Much of this increased capacity, as a result of indemnity pressures and heavy price controls, was extremely inefficient. We would expect, therefore, that as payments were completed and controls relaxed the efficiency or productivity of these industries would decline.

Considered from the viewpoint that outputs enter the system as inputs, less output from 16 of the 39 sectors was required in 1956 than in 1952 in effecting a unit increase in final demand for the output of each industry; that is, the efficiency of 16 outputs increased while that of the remaining 23 either declined or remained constant. The greatest relative increases occurred in the outputs of electrical and transport equipment, and printing and publishing, while the greatest relative decline occurred in the output of forestry, chemical products, and products of the basic metal industries.

B

INPUT-OUTPUT MATRICES INCLUDING INVERSES, 1952–56

Appendix Tables B–1, B–2, and B–3 were taken from *Panos-Tuotos-Tutkimus Suomen Talousilämästä Vuonna 1956* (Input-Output Study for Finland in 1956) by Osmo Forssell and Paavo Grönlund.

Appendix Tables B–4 and B–5 were compiled by the author from information obtained from (1) the abovementioned study, and (2) the Central Statistical Office of Finland, Helsinki.

TABLE B–1

Interindustry Flow of Goods and Services by Industry of Origin and Destination in Finland, 1956

(1,000 Million mk)

Producing Sector	Purchasing Sector	Agriculture	Hunting and fishing	Forestry	Mining and quarrying
		1	2	3	4
Agriculture	1	89.50	—	6.43	—
Hunting and fishing	2	0.13	—	—	—
Forestry	3	2.52	—	—	0.04
Mining and quarrying	4	0.05	—	—	0.35
Food manufacturing industries	5	12.92	—	—	—
Beverage industries	6	—	—	—	—
Tobacco manufactures	7	—	—	—	—
Manufacture of textiles	8	—	—	—	—
Manufacture of footwear, other wearing apparel, and made-up textile goods	9	—	—	—	—
Manufacture of wood and cork, except manufacture of furniture	10	—	—	—	0.02
Manufacture of furniture and fixtures	11	—	—	—	—
Manufacture of paper and paper products	12	—	—	—	0.17
Printing, publishing, and allied industries	13	—	—	—	0.02
Manufacture of leather and leather products, except footwear	14	—	—	—	—
Manufacture of rubber products	15	—	—	—	—
Manufacture of chemicals and chemical products	16	8.27	—	—	1.57
Manufacture of products of petroleum and asphalt	17	0.03	—	—	—
Manufacture of nonmetallic mineral products	18	0.03	—	—	—
Basic metal industries	19	—	—	—	—
Manufacture of metal products, except machinery and transport equipment	20	0.48	—	—	—
Manufacture of machinery, except electrical machinery	21	1.01	—	0.50	0.44
Manufacture of electrical machinery, apparatus, appliances, and supplies	22	0.20	—	—	0.19
Manufacture of transport equipment	23	0.80	0.13	—	—
Miscellaneous industries	24	0.12	—	—	—
House construction	25	2.99	—	0.48	0.11
Other construction and work	26	—	—	0.45	0.12
Electricity, gas, steam, and water services	27	1.54	—	0.01	0.59
Trade	28	5.82	0.05	0.01	0.09
Banking and insurance	29	2.35	—	0.01	0.08
Railway transport	30	1.39	—	0.01	0.01
Tramway and bus transport	31	—	—	—	—
Other road transport	32	2.21	—	0.01	0.27
Water transport	33	0.47	0.01	0.09	0.04
Air transport	34	0.02	—	—	—
Services incidental to transport	35	0.05	—	—	—
Communication	36	0.25	0.03	0.10	0.04
Central government	37	0.17	—	0.06	0.06
Local authorities	38	0.01	—	0.01	—
Other services	39	1.51	—	—	0.02
Total produced inputs		134.84	0.22	8.17	4.23
Labor incomes		94.23	4.03	52.15	3.18
Capital revenue		11.58	0.45	40.85	1.02
Depreciation		8.40	0.29	0.45	0.37
Indirect taxes minus subsidies		−4.19	—	0.03	0.52
Import		7.71	0.10	0.07	0.36
Total primary inputs		117.73	4.87	93.55	5.45
Undistributed		—	—	0.26	0.06
Total production		252.57	5.09	101.98	9.74

Food manuf. ind.	Beverage ind.	Tobacco manufactures	Manuf. of textiles	Manuf. of footwear, etc.	Manuf. of wood, etc.	Manuf. of furniture, etc.	Manuf. of paper, etc.
5	6	7	8	9	10	11	12
95.20	0.74	—	0.25	—	—	—	—
0.10	—	—	—	0.09	—	—	—
0.67	0.04	—	0.10	0.05	32.05	0.03	29.21
0.01	0.01	—	—	—	—	—	1.30
42.41	0.31	—	—	—	—	—	—
0.03	2.02	—	—	—	—	—	—
—	—	0.08	—	—	—	—	—
—	—	—	5.18	16.62	—	0.57	0.05
—	—	—	0.37	1.11	—	—	—
0.67	0.16	0.09	0.06	0.11	4.97	3.85	1.84
—	—	—	—	—	—	0.37	—
3.00	—	0.77	0.55	0.48	0.23	0.23	42.01
1.09	0.23	0.34	0.29	0.27	0.15	0.26	0.30
—	—	—	—	4.82	—	—	—
—	—	—	0.01	0.51	—	0.01	—
2.23	0.27	0.01	1.96	0.14	0.55	0.56	4.31
0.01	—	—	0.01	—	0.02	—	0.03
—	1.06	—	—	—	0.02	—	—
—	—	—	—	—	—	0.05	—
1.15	0.11	—	—	0.35	0.16	0.51	0.08
0.15	0.02	—	—	—	0.42	0.04	1.39
—	—	—	—	—	—	—	0.31
0.05	—	—	—	—	—	—	—
0.15	—	0.03	0.09	0.20	—	—	—
0.97	0.08	0.01	0.28	0.12	0.43	0.13	0.95
—	—	—	—	—	—	—	—
1.73	0.20	0.02	0.78	0.23	2.10	0.36	16.47
3.18	0.08	0.02	0.40	0.64	0.10	0.10	0.23
1.21	0.07	0.02	0.35	0.35	1.08	0.40	2.89
1.06	0.08	0.03	0.39	0.44	0.68	0.11	1.49
—	—	—	—	—	—	—	—
4.14	0.45	0.03	0.35	0.34	2.21	0.15	3.25
1.96	0.07	0.10	0.96	0.26	0.29	0.05	0.75
—	—	—	—	—	—	—	—
0.17	0.01	0.01	0.10	0.02	0.01	—	0.03
0.18	0.02	0.01	0.22	0.19	0.17	0.05	0.23
0.13	0.02	—	0.01	0.01	0.02	0.01	0.04
0.14	0.01	—	—	—	—	—	—
0.70	0.09	0.30	0.31	0.18	0.09	0.04	0.23
162.49	6.15	1.87	13.02	27.53	45.75	7.88	107.39
19.50	1.75	0.82	15.96	16.28	16.73	5.98	22.93
3.91	0.32	0.15	3.94	2.53	−1.78	0.88	12.35
2.73	0.27	0.05	1.38	0.45	2.06	0.32	2.62
5.90	1.06	0.34	1.13	0.91	0.44	0.22	1.14
28.41	1.01	1.63	14.68	4.24	1.33	0.83	3.45
60.45	4.41	2.99	37.09	24.41	18.78	8.23	42.49
0.04	0.41	—	3.82	2.25	—	0.16	2.50
222.98	10.97	4.86	53.93	54.19	64.53	16.27	152.38

TABLE B-1—*Continued*

Producing Sector	Purchasing Sector	Printing publishing, etc.	Manuf. of leather, etc.	Manuf. of rubber products	Manuf. of chemicals, etc.
		13	14	15	16
Agriculture	1	—	—	—	0.39
Hunting and fishing	2	—	—	—	—
Forestry	3	0.02	0.02	0.01	0.07
Mining and quarrying	4	—	—	—	0.32
Food manufacturing industries	5	—	0.63	—	0.19
Beverage industries	6	—	—	—	0.11
Tobacco manufactures	7	—	—	—	—
Manufacture of textiles	8	0.08	0.09	0.73	0.03
Manufacture of footwear, other wearing apparel, and made-up textile goods	9	—	—	—	—
Manufacture of wood and cork, except manufacture of furniture	10	—	—	0.02	0.05
Manufacture of furniture and fixtures	11	—	—	—	—
Manufacture of paper and paper products	12	4.34	0.34	0.12	2.05
Printing, publishing, and allied industries	13	8.51	0.02	0.06	0.50
Manufacture of leather and leather products, except footwear	14	0.02	0.33	—	—
Manufacture of rubber products	15	—	0.01	0.52	—
Manufacture of chemicals and chemical products	16	0.27	0.10	0.13	5.47
Manufacture of products of petroleum and asphalt	17	—	—	—	0.01
Manufacture of nonmetallic mineral products	18	—	—	—	0.57
Basic metal industries	19	—	—	—	0.01
Manufacture of metal products, except machinery and transport equipment	20	—	—	0.01	0.77
Manufacture of machinery, except electrical machinery	21	0.01	0.05	—	0.09
Manufacture of electrical machinery, apparatus, appliances, and supplies	22	—	—	—	0.03
Manufacture of transport equipment	23	—	—	—	0.08
Miscellaneous industries	24	—	—	—	0.03
House construction	25	0.14	0.03	0.07	0.25
Other construction and work	26	—	—	—	—
Electricity, gas, steam, and water services	27	0.18	0.06	0.20	1.42
Trade	28	0.11	0.07	0.07	0.38
Banking and insurance	29	0.27	0.07	0.10	0.23
Railway transport	30	0.09	0.05	0.05	0.26
Tramway and bus transport	31	—	—	—	—
Other road transport	32	0.20	0.09	0.08	0.32
Water transport	33	0.03	0.10	0.12	0.73
Air transport	34	—	—	—	0.02
Services incidental to transport	35	—	0.01	0.01	0.07
Communication	36	0.10	0.02	0.03	0.19
Central government	37	0.01	—	—	—
Local authorities	38	—	—	—	—
Other services	39	0.41	0.02	0.03	0.13
Total produced inputs		14.79	2.11	2.36	14.77
Labor incomes		10.03	1.69	2.34	5.86
Capital revenue		1.98	0.48	1.60	3.63
Depreciation		0.58	0.14	0.22	1.04
Indirect taxes minus subsidies		0.17	0.08	0.14	1.29
Import		0.28	1.50	2.08	11.19
Total primary inputs		13.04	3.89	6.38	23.01
Undistributed		0.89	0.32	0.37	3.45
Total production		28.72	6.32	9.11	41.23

Manuf. of petroleum, etc.	Manuf. of nonmet. mineral pr.	Basic metal ind.	Manuf. of metal pr., etc.	Manuf. of machinery etc.	Manuf. of elec. mach., etc.	Manuf. of transport equipm.	Misc. manuf. ind.
17	18	19	20	21	22	23	24
—	—	—	—	—	—	—	—
—	—	—	—	—	—	—	—
—	0.32	0.03	0.07	0.11	—	0.19	0.01
0.11	1.56	2.36	—	—	—	—	0.10
—	—	—	—	—	—	—	—
—	—	—	—	—	—	—	—
—	—	—	—	—	—	—	—
—	—	—	0.09	0.02	0.03	0.17	0.02
—	—	—	—	—	—	—	—
—	0.25	0.02	0.14	0.31	0.03	0.60	0.21
—	—	—	—	0.04	0.35	—	—
0.23	0.59	0.04	0.26	0.20	0.32	0.19	0.07
—	0.16	0.04	0.10	0.13	0.29	0.11	0.05
—	—	—	0.03	0.07	—	0.06	0.01
—	—	—	0.04	0.11	—	0.17	0.01
0.04	0.80	0.69	0.51	0.91	0.27	0.39	0.25
0.03	0.01	0.01	0.01	0.02	0.01	0.02	—
—	1.59	—	0.03	0.09	0.28	0.04	0.03
—	0.32	17.29	3.04	4.13	3.62	1.81	0.45
—	0.08	0.60	1.61	1.54	0.88	1.62	0.06
—	0.02	0.11	0.03	2.19	0.38	3.47	0.08
—	—	0.05	0.34	1.96	1.59	2.55	0.01
—	—	0.02	—	—	—	0.66	—
—	—	—	0.01	0.03	—	0.05	0.20
0.01	0.40	0.17	0.10	0.20	0.18	0.15	0.04
—	—	—	—	—	—	—	—
0.02	0.97	0.86	0.49	0.70	0.30	0.49	0.12
0.02	0.38	0.21	0.24	0.34	0.23	0.28	0.11
0.02	0.32	0.18	0.16	0.20	0.12	0.24	0.03
0.16	0.67	0.36	0.16	0.28	0.17	0.17	0.04
—	—	—	—	—	—	—	—
0.02	2.91	0.12	0.41	0.55	0.17	0.57	0.03
0.05	0.21	0.32	0.38	0.48	0.28	0.65	0.07
—	—	—	—	0.02	—	—	—
0.01	0.02	0.03	0.03	0.04	0.03	0.06	0.01
—	0.08	0.09	0.09	0.16	0.07	0.13	—
—	0.01	0.02	0.03	0.05	0.03	0.03	0.04
—	—	—	0.01	0.01	0.01	0.01	—
0.01	0.07	0.09	0.04	0.11	0.08	0.12	0.02
0.73	11.74	23.71	8.45	15.00	9.72	15.00	2.07
0.28	9.36	3.96	9.13	15.74	6.59	16.88	3.30
0.07	1.52	1.17	1.85	2.46	1.92	3.03	0.58
0.04	1.33	0.52	0.62	1.43	0.66	0.91	0.18
0.10	0.62	0.36	0.67	0.72	0.42	1.21	0.11
0.75	2.42	4.25	5.48	6.67	4.20	8.91	1.10
1.24	15.25	10.26	17.75	27.02	13.79	30.94	5.27
0.10	0.03	2.28	0.48	1.88	0.25	−0.14	0.54
2.07	27.02	36.25	26.68	43.90	23.76	45.80	7.88

TABLE B-1—*Continued*

Producing Sector	Purchasing Sector	House construction	Other construction	Electricity, etc.	Trade
		25	26	27	28
Agriculture	1	1.24	—	—	—
Hunting and fishing	2	—	—	—	—
Forestry	3	0.82	0.65	0.98	—
Mining and quarrying	4	0.54	0.37	0.16	—
Food manufacturing industries	5	—	—	0.03	—
Beverage industries	6	—	—	—	—
Tobacco manufactures	7	—	—	—	—
Manufacture of textiles	8	0.05	—	0.08	—
Manufacture of footwear, other wearing apparel, and made-up textile goods	9	—	—	0.01	—
Manufacture of wood and cork, except manufacture of furniture	10	6.61	4.03	3.26	—
Manufacture of furniture and fixtures	11	3.37	—	—	—
Manufacture of paper and paper products	12	1.14	1.18	0.18	2.27
Printing, publishing, and allied industries	13	—	—	0.14	2.62
Manufacture of leather and leather products, except footwear	14	—	—	0.02	—
Manufacture of rubber products	15	0.25	—	—	—
Manufacture of chemicals and chemical products	16	1.52	1.14	0.40	—
Manufacture of products of petroleum and asphalt	17	0.97	0.41	0.01	—
Manufacture of nonmetallic mineral products	18	14.60	5.67	0.06	—
Basic metal industries	19	2.62	1.13	0.02	—
Manufacture of metal products, except machinery and transport equipment	20	5.24	1.80	0.01	—
Manufacture of machinery, except electrical machinery	21	2.49	0.94	0.19	0.04
Manufacture of electrical machinery, apparatus, appliances, and supplies	22	1.71	2.58	0.04	0.13
Manufacture of transport equipment	23	1.24	0.76	0.05	—
Miscellaneous industries	24	0.18	0.37	—	—
House construction	25	—	—	0.73	1.30
Other construction and work	26	—	—	2.05	—
Electricity, gas, steam, and water services	27	0.59	0.06	27.56	0.36
Trade	28	6.80	2.27	0.60	4.29
Banking and insurance	29	0.67	0.25	2.09	4.41
Railway transport	30	1.47	0.58	0.21	—
Tramway and bus transport	31	—	—	—	—
Other road transport	32	8.82	11.15	0.56	8.95
Water transport	33	0.59	0.06	0.05	—
Air transport	34	—	—	—	—
Services incidental to transport	35	0.06	0.05	0.05	—
Communication	36	0.47	0.30	0.15	2.95
Central government	37	0.01	—	0.02	0.07
Local authorities	38	—	—	—	0.08
Other services	39	3.86	1.93	0.11	1.87
Total produced inputs		67.93	37.68	39.82	29.34
Labor incomes		59.66	32.76	8.24	63.23
Capital revenue		3.66	2.10	8.65	30.00
Depreciation		0.63	0.64	4.93	3.60
Indirect taxes minus subsidies		15.24	3.17	0.78	1.77
Import		7.02	1.57	7.27	—
Total primary inputs		86.21	40.24	29.87	98.60
Undistributed		0.16	0.02	1.34	—
Total production		154.30	77.94	71.03	127.94

Banking and insurance	Railway transport	Tramway and bus transp.	Other road transp.	Water transport	Air transport	Services incidental to transp.
29	30	31	32	33	34	35
—	0.11	—	—	—	—	—
—	—	—	—	—	—	—
—	1.51	—	—	0.04	—	0.06
—	0.11	—	—	—	—	—
—	—	—	—	—	—	—
—	—	—	—	—	—	—
—	—	—	—	—	—	—
—	—	—	—	0.13	—	—
—	—	—	—	0.06	—	—
—	—	—	—	—	—	—
—	0.07	—	—	—	—	—
0.14	0.01	—	0.01	—	—	0.01
0.15	0.05	0.08	—	0.02	0.01	0.05
—	—	—	—	—	—	—
—	—	0.20	1.17	—	—	—
—	0.05	—	—	0.06	—	—
—	0.02	0.06	0.26	—	—	—
—	—	—	—	—	—	—
—	—	—	—	—	—	—
—	—	—	—	—	—	—
—	—	—	—	0.03	—	—
—	—	—	—	—	—	—
—	3.09	2.46	9.06	1.53	0.48	—
—	—	—	—	—	—	—
0.43	1.19	0.10	0.10	0.01	—	0.01
—	2.48	—	—	0.31	—	—
0.11	0.20	0.23	0.02	0.02	—	0.01
0.18	0.20	0.42	3.18	0.06	0.01	0.05
—	0.01	0.35	0.83	0.80	0.03	0.05
0.11	1.15	0.09	0.54	0.11	0.02	0.16
0.27	—	—	—	—	—	—
0.27	0.21	0.23	1.40	0.11	0.03	0.23
0.01	0.11	0.08	0.17	0.99	—	0.10
0.02	—	—	—	—	—	0.05
—	—	—	—	0.13	0.02	—
0.47	0.07	0.04	0.08	0.35	0.03	0.07
0.02	—	—	—	0.10	0.04	—
—	—	—	—	—	—	—
0.83	0.07	0.05	—	0.05	0.01	0.05
3.01	11.07	4.39	16.82	4.91	0.68	0.90
10.37	14.95	4.95	30.74	10.39	0.48	1.53
13.51	—	0.13	2.35	6.16	0.08	0.86
0.43	0.80	2.13	4.97	2.26	0.15	0.11
0.07	−1.80	1.31	10.20	0.17	—	—
5.07	1.94	0.94	3.16	10.26	0.39	0.05
29.45	15.89	9.46	51.42	29.24	1.10	2.55
−0.05	—	0.35	0.02	—	0.04	0.01
32.41	26.96	14.20	68.26	34.15	1.82	3.46

TABLE B-1—*Continued*

Producing Sector	Purchasing Sector	Communication	Central government	Local authorities	Other services
		36	37	38	39
Agriculture	1	—	—	1.47	—
Hunting and fishing	2	—	—	—	—
Forestry	3	0.07	0.62	1.27	4.47
Mining and quarrying	4	—	0.02	—	0.36
Food manufacturing industries	5	—	1.01	2.62	—
Beverage industries	6	—	0.09	0.21	—
Tobacco manufactures	7	—	—	—	—
Manufacture of textiles	8	—	0.13	0.30	—
Manufacture of footwear other wearng apparel, and made-up textile goods	9	—	0.22	0.77	—
Manufacture of wood and cork, except manufacture of furniture	10	—	0.12	0.12	0.55
Manufacture of furniture and fixtures	11	—	0.50	0.60	—
Manufacture of paper and paper products	12	—	0.30	0.38	0.68
Printing, publishing, and allied industries	13	0.07	0.63	1.41	1.00
Manufacture of leather and leather products, except footwear	14	—	0.02	0.04	—
Manufacture of rubber products	15	—	0.05	0.08	—
Manufacture of chemicals and chemical products	16	—	0.25	0.03	0.22
Manufacture of products of petroleum and asphalt	17	—	0.03	—	—
Manufacture of nonmetallic mineral products	18	—	0.13	0.31	—
Basic metal industries	19	—	0.07	0.06	—
Manufacture of metal products, except machinery and transport equipment	20	0.01	0.24	0.29	—
Manufacture of machinery, except electrical machinery	21	0.14	0.51	0.69	0.04
Manufacture of electrical machinery, apparatus, appliances, and supplies	22	0.51	0.15	0.47	0.10
Manufacture of transport equipment	23	—	0.42	0.31	—
Miscellaneous industries	24	0.09	0.27	0.33	0.14
House construction	25	0.34	1.89	3.11	6.74
Other construction and work	26	0.93	6.14	3.39	—
Electricity, gas, steam, and water services	27	0.25	0.81	1.56	3.02
Trade	28	0.08	1.03	3.30	1.70
Banking and insurance	29	0.14	0.33	1.61	5.11
Railway transport	30	0.34	0.38	—	0.29
Tramway and bus transport	31	0.47	—	—	—
Other road transport	32	0.11	0.64	1.00	0.32
Water transport	33	0.02	—	—	0.17
Air transport	34	0.01	—	—	—
Services incidental to transport	35	—	—	—	0.02
Communication	36	0.27	1.22	0.61	0.51
Central government	37	0.01	—	0.57	0.02
Local authorities	38	—	—	—	—
Other services	39	0.12	0.44	0.68	1.67
Total produced inputs		3.98	18.66	27.59	27.13
Labor incomes		10.46	40.57	40.14	30.25
Capital revenue		0.78	1.97	4.93	30.39
Depreciation		1.07	0.50	1.64	8.73
Indirect taxes minus subsidies		0.37	—	0.71	1.49
Import		0.41	4.58	1.66	1.26
Total primary inputs		13.09	47.62	49.08	72.12
Undistributed		0.01	2.49	2.18	0.01
Total production		17.08	68.77	78.85	99.26

Total intermediate use	Gross capital formation	Consumption	Export	Total final demand	Undistributed	Total production
195.33	—	56.44	0.80	57.24	—	252.57
0.32	—	4.77	—	4.77	—	5.09
76.05	—	12.43	13.50	25.93	—	101.98
7.73	—	—	2.01	2.01	—	9.74
60.12	—	154.04	8.82	162.86	—	222.98
2.46	—	8.51	—	8.51	—	10.97
0.08	—	4.78	—	4.78	—	4.86
24.37	0.29	28.91	0.36	29.56	—	53.93
2.54	0.16	51.40	0.09	51.65	—	54.19
28.09	0.08	0.29	39.36	39.73	−3.29	64.53
5.30	3.94	5.66	1.37	10.97	—	16.27
62.49	—	11.24	80.77	92.01	−2.12	152.38
19.15	—	9.35	0.12	9.47	0.10	28.72
5.42	0.26	0.57	0.07	0.90	—	6.32
3.14	—	5.92	0.05	5.97	—	9.11
33.37	—	5.53	2.33	7.86	—	41.23
1.98	—	0.09	—	0.09	—	2.07
24.51	—	1.95	0.56	2.51	—	27.02
34.62	0.09	—	1.54	1.63	—	36.25
17.60	5.85	2.10	1.13	9.08	—	26.68
15.47	21.53	2.50	5.40	29.43	−1.00	43.90
12.92	6.00	3.18	1.66	10.84	—	23.76
21.14	8.68	2.48	13.50	24.66	—	45.80
2.29	0.43	5.01	0.15	5.59	—	7.88
24.24	130.06	—	—	130.06	—	154.30
15.87	59.88	—	—	59.88	2.19	77.94
64.64	—	6.39	—	6.39	—	71.03
37.33	7.05	82.91	0.65	90.61	—	127.94
27.43	0.13	2.12	2.78	5.03	−0.05	32.41
13.96	0.58	6.57	5.90	13.05	−0.05	26.96
0.74	—	13.46	—	13.46	—	14.20
52.91	0.39	8.73	4.15	13.27	2.08	68.26
10.82	3.09	2.24	18.00	23.33	—	34.15
0.14	—	1.11	0.57	1.68	—	1.82
1.05	0.30	0.80	1.31	2.41	—	3.46
10.04	—	7.05	0.09	7.14	−0.10	17.08
1.61	—	65.93	1.23	67.16	—	68.77
0.29	—	78.56	—	78.56	—	78.85
16.34	0.31	82.46	0.15	82.92	—	99.26
933.90	249.10	735.48	208.42	1,193.00	−2.24	2,124.66
697.42	—	—	—	—	—	697.42
202.06	—	—	—	—	—	202.06
59.65	—	—	—	—	—	59.65
46.87	15.45	49.76	−4.41	60.80	—	107.67
158.23	41.61	23.32	—	64.93	−2.01	221.15
1,164.23	57.06	73.08	−4.41	125.73	−2.01	1,287.95
26.53	—	—	—	—	—	26.53
2,124.66	306.16	808.56	204.01	1,318.73	−4.25	3,439.14

TABLE B–2

Coefficients of Production

1956

Producing sector	Purchasing sector	Agri- culture	Hunting and fishing	Forestry
		1	2	3
Agriculture	1	0.3543	—	0.0630
Hunting and fishing	2	0.0005	—	—
Forestry	3	0.0100	—	—
Mining and quarrying	4	0.0002	—	—
Food manufacturing industries	5	0.0512	—	—
Beverage industries	6	—	—	—
Tobacco manufactures	7	—	—	—
Manufacture of textiles	8	—	—	—
Manufacture of footwear, other wearing apparel, and made-up textile goods	9	—	—	—
Manufacture of wood and cork, except manufacture of furniture	10	—	—	—
Manufacture of furniture and fixtures	11	—	—	—
Manufacture of paper and paper products	12	—	—	—
Printing, publishing, and allied industries	13	—	—	—
Manufacture of leather and leather products, except footwear	14	—	—	—
Manufacture of rubber products	15	—	—	—
Manufacture of chemicals and chemical products	16	0.0327	—	—
Manufacture of products of petroleum and asphalt	17	0.0001	—	—
Manufacture of nonmetallic mineral products	18	0.0001	—	—
Basic metal industries	19	—	—	—
Manufacture of metal products, except machinery and transport equipment	20	0.0019	—	—
Manufacture of machinery, except electrical machinery	21	0.0040	—	0.0049
Manufacture of electrical machinery, apparatus, appliances, and supplies	22	0.0008	—	—
Manufacture of transport equipment	23	0.0032	0.0255	—
Miscellaneous industries	24	0.0005	—	—
House construction	25	0.0118	—	0.0047
Other construction and work	26	—	—	0.0044
Electricity, gas, steam, and water services	27	0.0061	—	0.0001
Trade	28	0.0230	0.0098	0.0001
Banking and insurance	29	0.0093	—	0.0001
Railway transport	30	0.0056	—	0.0001
Tramway and bus transport	31	—	—	—
Other road transport	32	0.0087	—	0.0001
Water transport	33	0.0019	0.0020	0.0009
Air transport	34	0.0000	—	—
Services incidental to transport	35	0.0002	—	—
Communication	36	0.0010	0.0059	0.0010
Central government	37	0.0007	—	0.0006
Local authorities	38	0.0000	—	0.0001
Other services	39	0.0060	—	—
Total produced inputs		0.5338	0.0432	0.0801
Labor incomes		0.3731	0.7917	0.5113
Capital revenue		0.0459	0.0884	0.4006
Depreciation		0.0332	0.0570	0.0044
Indirect taxes minus subsidies		−0.0166	—	0.0003
Import		0.0306	0.0197	0.0007
Total primary inputs		0.4662	0.9568	0.9173
Undistributed		—	—	0.0026
Total		1.0000	1.0000	1.0000

Mining and quarrying	Food manuf. ind.	Beverage industries	Tobacco manu- factures	Manuf. of textiles	Manuf. of footwear, etc.	Manuf. of wood, etc.
4	5	6	7	8	9	10
—	0.4269	0.0674	—	0.0046	—	—
—	0.0004	—	—	—	0.0016	—
0.0041	0.0030	0.0036	—	0.0018	0.0009	0.4966
0.0359	0.0001	0.0009	—	—	—	—
—	0.1902	0.0282	—	—	—	—
—	0.0001	0.1842	—	—	—	—
—	—	—	0.0164	—	—	—
—	—	—	—	0.0961	0.3067	—
—	—	—	—	0.0069	0.0205	—
0.0020	0.0030	0.0145	0.0185	0.0011	0.0020	0.0770
—	—	—	—	—	—	—
0.0175	0.0135	—	0.1585	0.0102	0.0089	0.0036
0.0021	0.0049	0.0210	0.0699	0.0053	0.0050	0.0023
—	—	—	—	—	0.0889	—
—	—	—	—	0.0002	0.0094	—
0.1611	0.0100	0.0246	0.0021	0.0364	0.0026	0.0085
—	0.0000	—	—	0.0002	—	0.0004
—	—	0.0967	—	—	—	0.0003
—	—	—	—	—	—	—
—	0.0052	0.0100	—	—	0.0065	0.0024
0.0452	0.0006	0.0018	—	—	—	0.006
0.0195	—	—	—	—	—	—
—	0.0003	—	—	—	—	—
—	0.0006	—	0.0062	0.0016	0.0037	—
0.0113	0.0044	0.0073	0.0020	0.0052	0.0022	0.0066
0.0123	—	—	—	—	—	—
0.0606	0.0078	0.0182	0.0041	0.0145	0.0042	0.0326
0.0093	0.0142	0.0073	0.0041	0.0074	0.0118	0.0015
0.0082	0.0054	0.0064	0.0041	0.0065	0.0065	0.0167
0.0010	0.0048	0.0073	0.0062	0.0072	0.0081	0.0106
—	—	—	—	—	—	—
0.0277	0.0186	0.0410	0.0062	0.0065	0.0063	0.0342
0.0041	0.0088	0.0064	0.0205	0.0178	0.0048	0.0045
—	—	—	—	—	—	—
—	0.0007	0.0009	0.0021	0.0019	0.0004	0.0002
0.0041	0.0008	0.0019	0.0021	0.0040	0.0035	0.0026
0.0062	0.0006	0.0019	—	0.0002	0.0002	0.0003
—	0.0006	0.0009	—	—	—	—
0.0020	0.0032	0.0082	0.0617	0.0058	0.0033	0.0014
0.4342	0.7287	0.5606	0.3847	0.2414	0.5080	0.7089
0.3265	0.0874	0.1595	0.1687	0.2959	0.3004	0.2593
0.1048	0.0176	0.0292	0.0309	0.0731	0.0467	−0.0276
0.0379	0.0122	0.0246	0.0103	0.0256	0.0083	0.0319
0.0534	0.0265	0.0966	0.0700	0.0209	0.0168	0.0068
0.0370	0.1274	0.0921	0.3354	0.2722	0.0782	0.0207
0.5596	0.2711	0.4020	0.6153	0.6877	0.4504	0.2911
0.0062	0.0002	0.0374	—	0.0709	0.0416	—
1.0000	1.0000	1.0000	1.0000	1.0000	1.0000	1.0000

TABLE B-2—*Continued*

Producing sector	Purchasing sector	Manuf. of furniture, etc.	Manuf. of paper, etc.	Printing, publishing, etc.
		11	12	13
Agriculture	1	—	—	—
Hunting and fishing	2	—	—	—
Forestry	3	0.0018	0.1916	0.0006
Mining and quarrying	4	—	0.0086	—
Food manufacturing industries	5	—	—	—
Beverage industries	6	—	—	—
Tobacco manufactures	7	—	—	—
Manufacture of textiles	8	0.0350	0.0003	0.0028
Manufacture of footwear, other wearing apparel, and made-up textile goods	9	—	—	—
Manufacture of wood and cork, except manufacture of furniture	10	0.2367	0.0121	—
Manufacture of furniture and fixtures	11	0.0227	—	—
Manufacture of paper and paper products	12	0.0141	0.2757	0.1511
Printing, publishing, and allied industries	13	0.0160	0.0019	0.2964
Manufacture of leather and leather products, except footwear	14	—	—	0.0007
Manufacture of rubber products	15	0.0006	—	—
Manufacture of chemicals and chemical products	16	0.0345	0.0283	0.0094
Manufacture of products of petroleum and asphalt	17	—	0.0002	—
Manufacture of nonmetallic mineral products	18	—	—	—
Basic metal industries	19	0.0030	—	—
Manufacture of metal products, except machinery and transport equipment	20	0.0314	0.0005	—
Manufacture of machinery, except electrical machinery	21	0.0024	0.0092	0.0003
Manufacture of electrical machinery, apparatus, appliances, and supplies	22	—	0.0020	—
Manufacture of transport equipment	23	—	—	—
Miscellaneous industries	24	—	—	—
House construction	25	0.0080	0.0062	0.0049
Other construction and work	26	—	—	—
Electricity, gas, steam, and water services	27	0.0221	0.1081	0.0062
Trade	28	0.0062	0.0015	0.0039
Banking and insurance	29	0.0246	0.0190	0.0094
Railway transport	30	0.0067	0.0098	0.0031
Tramway and bus transport	31	—	—	—
Other road transport	32	0.0093	0.0213	0.0070
Water transport	33	0.0030	0.0049	0.0010
Air transport	34	—	—	—
Services incidental to transport	35	—	0.0002	—
Communication	36	0.0031	0.0015	0.0035
Central government	37	0.0006	0.0003	0.0003
Local authorities	38	—	—	—
Other services	39	0.0025	0.0015	0.0143
Total produced inputs		0.4843	0.7047	0.5149
Labor incomes		0.3675	0.1505	0.3493
Capital revenue		0.0541	0.0810	0.0689
Depreciation		0.0197	0.0172	0.0202
Indirect taxes minus subsidies		0.0135	0.0075	0.0059
Import		0.0510	0.0226	0.0098
Total primary inputs		0.5058	0.2788	0.4541
Undistributed		0.0099	0.0165	0.0310
Total		1.0000	1.0000	1.0000

Manuf. of leather, etc.	Manuf. of rubber products	Manuf. of chemicals, etc.	Manuf. of petroleum, etc.	Manuf. of nonmet. mineral pr.	Basic metal ind.	Manuf. of metal pr., etc.
14	15	16	17	18	19	20
—	—	0.0094	—	—	—	—
—	—	—	—	—	—	—
0.0032	0.0010	0.0017	—	0.0118	0.0008	0.0026
—	—	0.0078	0.0531	0.0577	0.0651	—
0.0997	—	0.0046	—	—	—	—
—	—	0.0026	—	—	—	—
—	—	—	—	—	—	—
0.0142	0.0802	0.0008	—	—	—	0.0033
—	—	—	—	—	—	—
—	0.0022	0.0012	—	0.0093	0.0005	0.0053
—	—	—	—	—	—	—
0.0538	0.0131	0.0497	0.1111	0.0218	0.0011	0.0097
0.0032	0.0066	0.0121	—	0.0059	0.0011	0.0038
0.0522	—	—	—	—	—	0.0011
0.0016	0.0571	—	—	—	—	0.0015
0.0158	0.0143	0.1327	0.0193	0.0296	0.0191	0.0191
—	—	0.0002	0.0145	0.0004	0.0003	0.0004
—	—	0.0139	—	0.0589	—	0.0011
—	—	0.0002	—	0.0118	0.4769	0.1140
—	0.0011	0.0187	—	0.0030	0.0166	0.0603
0.0079	—	0.0022	—	0.0007	0.0030	0.0011
—	—	0.0007	—	—	0.0014	0.0128
—	—	0.0019	—	—	0.0005	—
—	—	0.0008	—	—	—	0.0004
0.0047	0.0077	0.0060	0.0048	0.0148	0.0047	0.0037
—	—	—	—	—	—	—
0.0095	0.0219	0.0345	0.0097	0.0359	0.0237	0.0184
0.0111	0.0077	0.0092	0.0097	0.0141	0.0058	0.0090
0.0111	0.0110	0.0056	0.0097	0.0118	0.0050	0.0060
0.0079	0.0055	0.0063	0.0773	0.0248	0.0099	0.0060
—	—	—	—	—	—	—
0.0142	0.0087	0.0077	0.0097	0.1077	0.0033	0.0153
0.0158	0.0132	0.0177	0.0241	0.0078	0.0089	0.0143
—	—	0.0005	—	—	—	—
0.0016	0.0011	0.0017	0.0048	0.0007	0.0008	0.0011
0.0032	0.0033	0.0046	—	0.0030	0.0025	0.0034
—	—	—	—	0.0004	0.0005	0.0011
—	—	—	—	—	—	0.0004
0.0032	0.0033	0.0032	0.0048	0.0025	0.0025	0.0015
0.3339	0.2590	0.3582	0.3526	0.4344	0.6540	0.3167
0.2674	0.2569	0.1421	0.1353	0.3465	0.1093	0.3422
0.0759	0.1756	0.0881	0.0338	0.0562	0.0322	0.0693
0.0222	0.0241	0.0252	0.0193	0.0492	0.0144	0.0232
0.0127	0.0154	0.0313	0.0483	0.0230	0.0099	0.0252
0.2373	0.2283	0.2714	0.3623	0.0895	0.1173	0.2054
0.6155	0.7003	0.5581	0.5990	0.5644	0.2831	0.6653
0.0506	0.0407	0.0837	0.0484	0.0012	0.0629	0.0180
1.0000	1.0000	1.0000	1.0000	1.0000	1.0000	1.0000

TABLE B-2—*Continued*

Producing sector	Purchasing sector	Manuf. of machinery, etc.	Manuf. of elec. mach., etc.	Manuf. of transport equipm.
		21	22	23
Agriculture	1	—	—	—
Hunting and fishing	2	—	—	—
Forestry	3	0.0025	—	0.0041
Mining and quarrying	4	—	—	—
Food manufacturing industries	5	—	—	—
Beverage industries	6	—	—	—
Tobacco manufactures	7	—	—	—
Manufacture of textiles	8	0.0004	0.0013	0.0037
Manufacture of footwear, other wearing apparel, and made-up textile goods	9	—	—	—
Manufacture of wood and cork, except manufacture of furniture	10	0.0071	0.0013	0.0131
Manufacture of furniture and fixtures	11	0.0009	0.0147	—
Manufacture of paper and paper products	12	0.0045	0.0135	0.0042
Printing, publishing, and allied industries	13	0.0030	0.0122	0.0024
Manufacture of leather and leather products, except footwear	14	0.0016	—	0.0013
Manufacture of rubber products	15	0.0025	—	0.0037
Manufacture of chemicals and chemical products	16	0.0207	0.0113	0.0085
Manufacture of products of petroleum and asphalt	17	0.0005	0.0004	0.0004
Manufacture of nonmetallic mineral products	18	0.0020	0.0117	0.0009
Basic metal industries	19	0.0941	0.1524	0.0395
Manufacture of metal products, except machinery and transport equipment	20	0.0351	0.0370	0.0354
Manufacture of machinery, except electrical machinery	21	0.0499	0.0160	0.0758
Manufacture of electrical machinery, apparatus, appliances, and supplies	22	0.0446	0.0670	0.0556
Manufacture of transport equipment	23	—	—	0.0145
Miscellaneous industries	24	0.0007	—	0.0010
House construction	25	0.0046	0.0075	0.0033
Other construction and work	26	—	—	—
Electricity, gas, steam, and water services	27	0.0159	0.0127	0.0107
Trade	28	0.0078	0.0096	0.0061
Banking and insurance	29	0.0045	0.0051	0.0053
Railway transport	30	0.0064	0.0071	0.0037
Tramway and bus transport	31	—	—	—
Other road transport	32	0.0125	0.0071	0.0124
Water transport	33	0.0110	0.0118	0.0142
Air transport	34	0.0004	—	—
Services incidental to transport	35	0.0009	0.0013	0.0013
Communication	36	0.0037	0.0030	0.0029
Central government	37	0.0011	0.0013	0.0006
Local authorities	38	0.0002	0.0004	0.0002
Other services	39	0.0025	0.0033	0.0027
Total produced inputs		0.3416	0.4090	0.3275
Labor incomes		0.3586	0.2774	0.3685
Capital revenue		0.0560	0.0808	0.0662
Depreciation		0.0326	0.0278	0.0198
Indirect taxes minus subsidies		0.0164	0.0177	0.0265
Import		0.1519	0.1767	0.1945
Total primary inputs		0.6155	0.5804	0.6755
Undistributed		0.0429	0.0106	−0.0030
Total		1.0000	1.0000	1.0000

Misc. manuf. ind.	House construction	Other construction	Electricity, etc.	Trade	Banking and insurance	Railway transport
24	25	26	27	28	29	30
—	0.0080	—	—	—	—	0.0041
—	—	—	—	—	—	—
0.0013	0.0053	0.0083	0.0138	—	—	0.0560
0.0127	0.0035	0.0047	0.0023	—	—	0.0041
—	—	—	0.0004	—	—	—
—	—	—	—	—	—	—
—	—	—	—	—	—	—
0.0025	0.0003	—	0.0011	—	—	—
—	—	—	0.0001	—	—	—
0.0266	0.0429	0.0517	0.0459	—	—	—
—	0.0218	—	—	—	—	0.0026
0.0089	0.0074	0.0152	0.0025	0.0177	0.0043	0.0004
0.0063	—	—	0.0020	0.0205	0.0046	0.0018
0.0013	—	—	0.0003	—	—	—
0.0013	0.0016	—	—	—	—	—
0.0317	0.0099	0.0146	0.0056	—	—	0.0019
—	0.0062	0.0053	0.0001	—	—	0.0007
0.0038	0.0947	0.0727	0.0008	—	—	—
0.0571	0.0170	0.0145	0.0003	—	—	—
0.0076	0.0339	0.0231	0.0001	—	—	—
0.0101	0.0161	0.0121	0.0027	0.0003	—	—
0.0013	0.0111	0.0331	0.0006	0.0010	—	—
—	0.0081	0.0097	0.0007	—	—	0.1146
0.0254	0.0011	0.0048	—	—	—	—
0.0051	—	—	0.0103	0.0102	0.0133	0.0441
—	—	—	0.0289	—	—	0.0920
0.0152	0.0039	0.0007	0.3880	0.0028	0.0034	0.0074
0.0140	0.0440	0.0292	0.0084	0.0335	0.0056	0.0074
0.0038	0.0044	0.0032	0.0294	0.0345	—	0.0004
0.0051	0.0095	0.0074	0.0030	—	0.0034	0.0560
—	—	—	—	—	0.0083	—
0.0038	0.0572	0.1431	0.0079	0.0699	0.0083	0.0078
0.0089	0.0038	0.0007	0.0007	—	0.0003	0.0041
—	—	—	—	—	0.0006	—
0.0013	0.0004	0.0007	0.0007	—	—	—
—	0.0030	0.0038	0.0021	0.0231	0.0145	0.0026
0.0051	0.0001	—	0.0003	0.0005	0.0006	—
—	—	—	—	0.0007	—	—
0.0025	0.0250	0.0248	0.0015	0.0146	0.0256	0.0026
0.2627	0.4402	0.4834	0.5605	0.2293	0.0928	0.4106
0.4188	0.3866	0.4203	0.1160	0.4942	0.3200	0.5545
0.0736	0.0238	0.0270	0.1218	0.2345	0.4168	—
0.0229	0.0040	0.0082	0.0694	0.0281	0.0133	0.0297
0.0139	0.0988	0.0406	0.0110	0.0139	0.0022	−0.0668
0.1396	0.0455	0.0202	0.1024	—	0.1564	0.0720
0.6688	0.5587	0.5163	0.4206	0.7707	0.9087	0.5894
0.0685	0.0011	0.0003	0.0189	—	−0.0015	—
1.0000	1.0000	1.0000	1.0000	1.0000	1.0000	1.0000

TABLE B–2—*Continued*

Producing sector	Purchasing sector	Tramway and bus transp.	Other road transp.	Water transport
		31	32	33
Agriculture	1	—	—	—
Hunting and fishing	2	—	—	—
Forestry	3	—	—	0.0011
Mining and quarrying	4	—	—	—
Food manufacturing industries	5	—	—	—
Beverage industries	6	—	—	—
Tobacco manufactures	7	—	—	—
Manufacture of textiles	8	—	—	0.0038
Manufacture of footwear, other wearing apparel, and made-up textile goods	9	—	—	0.0018
Manufacture of wood and cork, except manufacture of furniture	10	—	—	—
Manufacture of furniture and fixtures	11	—	—	—
Manufacture of paper and paper products	12	—	0.0001	—
Printing, publishing, and allied industries	13	0.0056	—	0.0006
Manufacture of leather and leather products, except footwear	14	—	—	—
Manufacture of rubber products	15	0.0141	0.0171	—
Manufacture of chemicals and chemical products	16	—	—	0.0017
Manufacture of products of petroleum and asphalt	17	0.0042	0.0038	—
Manufacture of nonmetallic mineral products	18	—	—	—
Basic metal industries	19	—	—	—
Manufacture of metal products, except machinery and transport equipment	20	—	—	—
Manufacture of machinery, except electrical machinery	21	—	—	0.0009
Manufacture of electrical machinery, apparatus, appliances, and supplies	22	—	—	—
Manufacture of transport equipment	23	0.1732	0.1328	0.0448
Miscellaneous industries	24	—	—	—
House construction	25	0.0071	0.0014	0.0003
Other construction and work	26	—	—	0.0091
Electricity, gas, steam, and water services	27	0.0162	0.0003	0.0006
Trade	28	0.0296	0.0466	0.0017
Banking and insurance	29	0.0246	0.0122	0.0234
Railway transport	30	0.0063	0.0079	0.0033
Tramway and bus transport	31	—	—	—
Other road transport	32	0.0162	0.0205	0.0033
Water transport	33	0.0057	0.0025	0.0290
Air transport	34	—	—	—
Services incidental to transport	35	—	—	0.0038
Communication	36	0.0028	0.0012	0.0102
Central government	37	—	—	0.0030
Local authorities	38	—	—	—
Other services	39	0.0035	—	0.0014
Total produced inputs		0.3091	0.2464	0.1438
Labor incomes		0.3486	0.4503	0.3043
Capital revenue		0.0092	0.0344	0.1804
Depreciation		0.1500	0.0728	0.0061
Indirect taxes minus subsidies		0.0922	0.1495	0.0050
Import		0.0662	0.0463	0.3004
Total primary inputs		0.6662	0.7533	0.8562
Undistributed		0.0247	0.0003	—
Total		1.0000	1.0000	1.0000

Air transport	Services incidental to transp.	Communication	Central government	Local authorities	Other services
34	35	36	37	38	39
—	—	—	—	0.0186	—
—	—	—	—	—	—
—	0.0173	0.0040	0.0090	0.0161	0.0450
—	—	—	0.0003	—	0.0036
—	—	—	0.0146	0.0332	—
—	—	—	0.0014	0.0027	—
—	—	—	—	—	—
—	—	—	0.0018	0.0038	—
—	—	—	0.0032	0.0098	—
—	—	—	0.0018	0.0015	0.0056
—	—	—	0.0073	0.0076	—
—	0.0029	—	0.0043	0.0048	0.0068
0.0055	0.0144	0.0041	0.0092	0.0179	0.0101
—	—	—	0.0003	0.0005	—
—	—	—	0.0007	0.0010	—
—	—	—	0.0036	0.0004	0.0022
—	—	—	0.0005	—	—
—	—	—	0.0019	0.0039	—
—	—	—	0.0010	0.0008	—
—	—	0.0006	0.0035	0.0037	—
—	—	0.0082	0.0074	0.0087	0.0004
—	—	0.0299	0.0022	0.0060	0.0010
0.2637	—	—	0.0061	0.0039	—
—	—	0.0053	0.0039	0.0042	0.0014
—	0.0029	0.0199	0.0275	0.0394	0.0679
—	—	0.0544	0.0893	0.0430	—
—	0.0029	0.0147	0.0117	0.0198	0.0304
0.0055	0.0145	0.0046	0.0150	0.0419	0.0172
0.0165	0.0145	0.0082	0.0048	0.0204	0.0514
0.0110	0.0462	0.0199	0.0055	—	0.0030
—	—	0.0276	—	—	—
0.0165	0.0664	0.0064	0.0094	0.0127	0.0032
—	0.0289	0.0012	—	—	0.0017
—	0.0145	0.0006	—	—	—
0.0110	—	—	—	—	0.0002
0.0165	0.0202	0.0158	0.0177	0.0077	0.0051
0.0219	—	0.0005	—	0.0072	0.0002
—	—	—	—	—	—
0.0055	0.0145	0.0071	0.0064	0.0087	0.0169
0.3736	0.2601	0.2330	0.2713	0.3499	0.2733
0.2637	0.4422	0.6124	0.5899	0.5090	0.3048
0.0440	0.2485	0.0457	0.0287	0.0625	0.3062
0.0824	0.0318	0.0626	0.0072	0.0208	0.0879
—	—	0.0217	—	0.0090	0.0150
0.2143	0.0145	0.0240	0.0666	0.0211	0.0127
0.6044	0.7370	0.7664	0.6924	0.6224	0.7266
0.0220	0.0029	0.0006	0.0363	0.0277	0.0001
1.0000	1.0000	1.0000	1.0000	1.0000	1.0000

TABLE B–3

Inverse of the Identity Matrix Less the Matrix of Coefficients of Production 1956

Producing sector	Purchasing sector	Agri- culture	Hunting and fishing	Forestry
		1	2	3
Agriculture	1	1.6202	0.0001	0.1022
Hunting and fishing	2	0.0009	1.0000	0.0000
Forestry	3	0.0221	0.0006	1.0019
Mining and quarrying	4	0.0019	0.0003	0.0003
Food manufacturing industries	5	0.1029	0.0000	0.0065
Beverage industries	6	0.0002	0.0000	0.0000
Tobacco manufactures	7	0.0000	0.0000	0.0000
Manufacture of textiles	8	0.0003	0.0001	0.0000
Manufacture of footwear, other wearing apparel, and made-up textile goods	9	0.0000	0.0000	0.0000
Manufacture of wood and cork, except manufacture of furniture	10	0.0036	0.0005	0.0008
Manufacture of furniture and fixtures	11	0.0006	0.0000	0.0002
Manufacture of paper and paper products	12	0.0094	0.0007	0.0009
Printing, publishing, and allied industries	13	0.0039	0.0005	0.0004
Manufacture of leather and leather products, except footwear	14	0.0000	0.0000	0.0000
Manufacture of rubber products	15	0.0005	0.0001	0.0000
Manufacture of chemicals and chemical products	16	0.0644	0.0006	0.0045
Manufacture of products of petroleum and asphalt	17	0.0005	0.0000	0.0000
Manufacture of nonmetallic mineral products	18	0.0037	0.0001	0.0011
Basic metal industries	19	0.0059	0.0033	0.0020
Manufacture of metal products, except machinery and transport equipment	20	0.0070	0.0013	0.0010
Manufacture of machinery, except electrical machinery	21	0.0089	0.0022	0.0059
Manufacture of electrical machinery, apparatus, appliances, and supplies	22	0.0032	0.0019	0.0008
Manufacture of transport equipment	23	0.0106	0.0263	0.0010
Miscellaneous industries	24	0.0011	0.0000	0.0001
House construction	25	0.0229	0.0005	0.0063
Other construction and work	26	0.0024	0.0005	0.0047
Electricity, gas, steam and water services	27	0.0258	0.0012	0.0023
Trade	28	0.0441	0.0106	0.0034
Banking and insurance	29	0.0201	0.0008	0.0016
Railway transport	30	0.0119	0.0004	0.0011
Tramway and bus transport	31	0.0003	0.0002	0.0000
Other road transport	32	0.0236	0.0014	0.0003
Water transport	33	0.0062	0.0026	0.0015
Air transport	34	0.0000	0.0000	0.0000
Services incidental to transport	35	0.0006	0.0000	0.0000
Communication	36	0.0039	0.0064	0.0014
Central government	37	0.0013	0.0000	0.0007
Local authorities	38	0.0001	0.0000	0.0001
Other services	39	0.0126	0.0004	0.0011

Mining and quarrying	Food manuf. ind.	Beverage industries	Tobacco manu-factures	Manuf. of textiles	Manuf. of footwear, etc.	Manuf. of wood, etc.
4	5	6	7	8	9	10
0.0066	0.8560	0.1672	0.0073	0.0105	0.0127	0.0561
0.0000	0.0009	0.0001	0.0000	0.0000	0.0016	0.0000
0.0221	0.0250	0.0271	0.0662	0.0102	0.0122	0.5447
1.0416	0.0019	0.0106	0.0032	0.0011	0.0011	0.0010
0.0018	1.2894	0.0537	0.0006	0.0011	0.0128	0.0037
0.0006	0.0003	1.2260	0.0000	0.0002	0.0000	0.0000
0.0000	0.0000	0.0000	1.0167	0.0000	0.0000	0.0000
0.0007	0.0004	0.0006	0.0007	1.1093	0.3500	0.0003
0.0000	0.0000	0.0000	0.0000	0.0079	1.0234	0.0000
0.0122	0.0082	0.0256	0.0281	0.0042	0.0053	1.0880
0.0009	0.0005	0.0005	0.0003	0.0002	0.0002	0.0004
0.0438	0.0324	0.0191	0.2470	0.0222	0.0304	0.0088
0.0089	0.0121	0.0407	0.1038	0.0102	0.0121	0.0047
0.0002	0.0000	0.0001	0.0001	0.0008	0.0960	0.0000
0.0010	0.0008	0.0015	0.0004	0.0006	0.0108	0.0009
0.1995	0.0503	0.0511	0.0142	0.0489	0.0227	0.0148
0.0005	0.0004	0.0006	0.0002	0.0004	0.0002	0.0008
0.0067	0.0032	0.1290	0.0017	0.0018	0.0014	0.0024
0.0211	0.0063	0.0102	0.0032	0.0018	0.0037	0.0050
0.0089	0.0116	0.0170	0.0015	0.0017	0.0084	0.0048
0.0528	0.0067	0.0061	0.0042	0.0012	0.0021	0.0120
0.0264	0.0026	0.0024	0.0017	0.0009	0.0011	0.0018
0.0076	0.0113	0.0136	0.0050	0.0040	0.0046	0.0082
0.0004	0.0014	0.0003	0.0066	0.0020	0.0046	0.0001
0.0170	0.0195	0.0175	0.0110	0.0083	0.0074	0.0129
0.0182	0.0030	0.0042	0.0036	0.0025	0.0026	0.0059
0.1276	0.0370	0.0584	0.0588	0.0349	0.0264	0.0630
0.0181	0.0441	0.0229	0.0092	0.0113	0.0192	0.0074
0.0172	0.0206	0.0177	0.0170	0.0110	0.0138	0.0224
0.0056	0.0138	0.0169	0.0113	0.0101	0.0139	0.0142
0.0003	0.0003	0.0003	0.0003	0.0003	0.0003	0.0003
0.0409	0.0400	0.0752	0.0172	0.0114	0.0152	0.0426
0.0102	0.0154	0.0123	0.0240	0.0219	0.0145	0.0068
0.0001	0.0000	0.0000	0.0000	0.0000	0.0000	0.0000
0.0006	0.0013	0.0015	0.0024	0.0023	0.0014	0.0004
0.0073	0.0043	0.0051	0.0045	0.0058	0.0068	0.0046
0.0067	0.0016	0.0028	0.0003	0.0004	0.0004	0.0008
0.0000	0.0008	0.0012	0.0000	0.0000	0.0000	0.0000
0.0053	0.0119	0.0143	0.0671	0.0079	0.0074	0.0035

TABLE B-3—*Continued*

Producing sector	Purchasing sector	Manuf. of furniture, etc.	Manuf. of paper, etc.	Printing, publishing, etc.
		11	12	13
Agriculture	1	0.0162	0.0308	0.0076
Hunting and fishing	2	0.0000	0.0000	0.0000
Forestry	3	0.1436	0.2879	0.0657
Mining and quarrying	4	0.0023	0.0144	0.0036
Food manufacturing industries	5	0.0014	0.0024	0.0008
Beverage industries	6	0.0002	0.0002	0.0000
Tobacco manufactures	7	0.0000	0.0000	0.0000
Manufacture of textiles	8	0.0403	0.0011	0.0048
Manufacture of footwear, other wearing apparel, and made-up textile goods	9	0.0003	0.0000	0.0000
Manufacture of wood and cork, except manufacture of furniture	10	0.2676	0.0328	0.0088
Manufacture of furniture and fixtures	11	1.0236	0.0005	0.0004
Manufacture of paper and paper products	12	0.0328	1.3886	0.3005
Printing, publishing, and allied industries	13	0.0267	0.0066	1.1238
Manufacture of leather and leather products, except footwear	14	0.0001	0.0001	0.0011
Manufacture of rubber products	15	0.0013	0.0008	0.0004
Manufacture of chemicals and chemical products	16	0.0498	0.0527	0.0277
Manufacture of products of petroleum and asphalt	17	0.0004	0.0007	0.0003
Manufacture of nonmetallic mineral products	18	0.0028	0.0036	0.0021
Basic metal industries	19	0.0170	0.0076	0.0028
Manufacture of metal products, except machinery and transport equipment	20	0.0374	0.0042	0.0018
Manufacture of machinery, except electrical machinery	21	0.0070	0.0181	0.0050
Manufacture of electrical machinery, apparatus, appliances, and supplies	22	0.0020	0.0057	0.0019
Manufacture of transport equipment	23	0.0057	0.0085	0.0044
Miscellaneous industries	24	0.0002	0.0002	0.0002
House construction	25	0.0145	0.0159	0.0130
Other construction and work	26	0.0042	0.0108	0.0038
Electricity, gas, steam and water services	27	0.0648	0.2543	0.0724
Trade	28	0.0121	0.0098	0.0100
Banking and insurance	29	0.0350	0.0370	0.0238
Railway transport	30	0.0130	0.0176	0.0093
Tramway and bus transport	31	0.0005	0.0004	0.0004
Other road transport	32	0.0254	0.0393	0.0209
Water transport	33	0.0076	0.0096	0.0042
Air transport	34	0.0000	0.0000	0.0000
Services incidental to transport	35	0.0004	0.0007	0.0002
Communication	36	0.0061	0.0047	0.0069
Central government	37	0.0010	0.0009	0.0007
Local authorities	38	0.0000	0.0000	0.0000
Other services	39	0.0059	0.0051	0.0228

Manuf. of leather, etc.	Manuf. of rubber products	Manuf. of chemicals, etc.	Manuf. of petroleum, etc.	Manuf. of nonmet. mineral pr.	Basic metal ind.	Manuf. of metal pr., etc.
14	15	16	17	18	19	20
0.0931	0.0025	0.0256	0.0058	0.0058	0.0050	0.0031
0.0001	0.0000	0.0000	0.0000	0.0000	0.0000	0.0000
0.0253	0.0191	0.0259	0.0412	0.0335	0.0125	0.0139
0.0017	0.0009	0.0124	0.0588	0.0672	0.1314	0.0171
0.1360	0.0003	0.0084	0.0006	0.0007	0.0007	0.0006
0.0001	0.0000	0.0037	0.0001	0.0002	0.0002	0.0001
0.0000	0.0000	0.0000	0.0000	0.0000	0.0000	0.0000
0.0171	0.0946	0.0015	0.0005	0.0006	0.0006	0.0044
0.0002	0.0007	0.0000	0.0000	0.0000	0.0000	0.0000
0.0045	0.0063	0.0085	0.0068	0.0177	0.0083	0.0101
0.0003	0.0003	0.0003	0.0006	0.0006	0.0005	0.0005
0.0862	0.0257	0.0871	0.1621	0.0421	0.0146	0.0208
0.0078	0.0120	0.0219	0.0028	0.0119	0.0064	0.0082
1.0551	0.0001	0.0001	0.0000	0.0000	0.0001	0.0013
0.0023	1.0609	0.0005	0.0005	0.0024	0.0005	0.0022
0.0294	0.0236	1.1623	0.0408	0.0532	0.0702	0.0343
0.0002	0.0002	0.0005	1.0151	0.0012	0.0009	0.0007
0.0018	0.0017	0.0191	0.0029	1.0662	0.0034	0.0031
0.0042	0.0018	0.0094	0.0048	0.0308	1.9262	0.2399
0.0028	0.0025	0.0247	0.0027	0.0073	0.0374	1.0706
0.0113	0.0012	0.0058	0.0066	0.0075	0.0142	0.0044
0.0017	0.0009	0.0030	0.0035	0.0041	0.0081	0.0165
0.0064	0.0039	0.0076	0.0147	0.0219	0.0074	0.0056
0.0003	0.0002	0.0011	0.0002	0.0002	0.0002	0.0006
0.0098	0.0109	0.0111	0.0127	0.0214	0.0147	0.0079
0.0029	0.0027	0.0044	0.0109	0.0068	0.0074	0.0034
0.0386	0.0478	0.0868	0.0561	0.0842	0.0979	0.0512
0.0197	0.0117	0.0156	0.0154	0.0261	0.0174	0.0148
0.0186	0.0160	0.0138	0.0178	0.0208	0.0168	0.0120
0.0125	0.0083	0.0110	0.0866	0.0317	0.0228	0.0111
0.0003	0.0003	0.0003	0.0002	0.0003	0.0003	0.0003
0.0250	0.0141	0.0188	0.0218	0.1273	0.0174	0.0227
0.0206	0.0172	0.0231	0.0282	0.0118	0.0210	0.0196
0.0000	0.0000	0.0006	0.0001	0.0000	0.0000	0.0000
0.0020	0.0015	0.0022	0.0052	0.0011	0.0019	0.0016
0.0054	0.0051	0.0072	0.0024	0.0058	0.0075	0.0058
0.0003	0.0001	0.0003	0.0006	0.0010	0.0020	0.0016
0.0001	0.0000	0.0000	0.0000	0.0000	0.0000	0.0004
0.0063	0.0056	0.0059	0.0074	0.0055	0.0073	0.0037

TABLE B-3—*Continued*

Producing sector	Purchasing sector	Manuf. of machinery, etc.	Manuf. of elec. mach., etc.	Manuf. of transport equipm.
		21	22	23
Agriculture	1	0.0025	0.0025	0.0024
Hunting and fishing	2	0.0000	0.0000	0.0000
Forestry	3	0.0138	0.0140	0.0176
Mining and quarrying	4	0.0156	0.0241	0.0090
Food manufacturing industries	5	0.0007	0.0004	0.0005
Beverage industries	6	0.0001	0.0001	0.0000
Tobacco manufactures	7	0.0000	0.0000	0.0000
Manufacture of textiles	8	0.0014	0.0027	0.0052
Manufacture of footwear, other wearing apparel, and made-up textile goods	9	0.0000	0.0000	0.0000
Manufacture of wood and cork, except manufacture of furniture	10	0.0125	0.0105	0.0184
Manufacture of furniture and fixtures	11	0.0020	0.0166	0.0013
Manufacture of paper and paper products	12	0.0144	0.0307	0.0128
Printing, publishing, and allied industries	13	0.0077	0.0218	0.0068
Manufacture of leather and leather products, except footwear	14	0.0019	0.0001	0.0016
Manufacture of rubber products	15	0.0033	0.0005	0.0047
Manufacture of chemicals and chemical products	16	0.0364	0.0309	0.0200
Manufacture of products of petroleum and asphalt	17	0.0008	0.0008	0.0007
Manufacture of nonmetallic mineral products	18	0.0047	0.0150	0.0033
Basic metal industries	19	0.2166	0.3299	0.1222
Manufacture of metal products, except machinery and transport equipment	20	0.0468	0.0511	0.0471
Manufacture of machinery, except electrical machinery	21	1.0562	0.0219	0.0841
Manufacture of electrical machinery, apparatus, appliances, and supplies	22	0.0526	1.0755	0.0662
Manufacture of transport equipment	23	0.0054	0.0054	1.0195
Miscellaneous industries	24	0.0009	0.0002	0.0012
House construction	25	0.0091	0.0134	0.0072
Other construction and work	26	0.0033	0.0038	0.0025
Electricity, gas, steam and water services	27	0.0467	0.0502	0.0342
Trade	28	0.0139	0.0169	0.0115
Banking and insurance	29	0.0104	0.0128	0.0105
Railway transport	30	0.0118	0.0143	0.0081
Tramway and bus transport	31	0.0003	0.0003	0.0002
Other road transport	32	0.0204	0.0176	0.0198
Water transport	33	0.0167	0.0186	0.0195
Air transport	34	0.0005	0.0000	0.0000
Services incidental to transport	35	0.0014	0.0019	0.0018
Communication	36	0.0062	0.0060	0.0052
Central government	37	0.0016	0.0019	0.0011
Local authorities	38	0.0003	0.0005	0.0003
Other services	39	0.0049	0.0065	0.0048

Misc. manuf. ind.	House con- struction	Other con- struction	Elec- tricity, etc.	Trade	Banking and insurance	Railway trans- port
24	25	26	27	28	29	30
0.0026	0.0038	0.0180	0.0057	0.0083	0.0048	0.0007
0.0000	0.0000	0.0000	0.0000	0.0000	0.0000	0.0000
0.0237	0.0421	0.0483	0.0693	0.0090	0.0044	0.0700
0.0227	0.0145	0.0145	0.0055	0.0008	0.0005	0.0079
0.0008	0.0013	0.0006	0.0015	0.0001	0.0000	0.0011
0.0002	0.0000	0.0000	0.0000	0.0000	0.0000	0.0000
0.0000	0.0000	0.0000	0.0000	0.0000	0.0000	0.0000
0.0033	0.0019	0.0008	0.0023	0.0004	0.0001	0.0010
0.0000	0.0000	0.0000	0.0002	0.0000	0.0000	0.0000
0.0332	0.0567	0.0605	0.0861	0.0023	0.0018	0.0125
0.0003	0.0228	0.0008	0.0006	0.0004	0.0004	0.0042
0.0209	0.0215	0.0312	0.0115	0.0331	0.0085	0.0079
0.0117	0.0052	0.0046	0.0067	0.0314	0.0075	0.0048
0.0015	0.0001	0.0001	0.0006	0.0000	0.0000	0.0002
0.0017	0.0034	0.0032	0.0006	0.0015	0.0004	0.0012
0.0473	0.0244	0.0281	0.0153	0.0024	0.0011	0.0105
0.0002	0.0068	0.0062	0.0007	0.0004	0.0002	0.0018
0.0061	0.1024	0.0793	0.0076	0.0017	0.0018	0.0132
0.1191	0.0546	0.0546	0.0071	0.0030	0.0016	0.0233
0.0127	0.0414	0.0305	0.0036	0.0014	0.0010	0.0111
0.0138	0.0213	0.0185	0.0078	0.0023	0.0010	0.0139
0.0036	0.0158	0.0398	0.0043	0.0031	0.0011	0.0131
0.0035	0.0217	0.0343	0.0069	0.0111	0.0040	0.1299
1.0262	0.0013	0.0051	0.0003	0.0002	0.0002	0.0008
0.0088	1.0077	0.0072	0.0204	0.0138	0.0162	0.0499
0.0032	0.0033	1.0030	0.0491	0.0022	0.0016	0.0992
0.0428	0.0302	0.0252	1.6447	0.0139	0.0099	0.2279
0.0187	0.0548	0.0430	0.0196	1.0404	0.0083	0.0176
0.0091	0.0145	0.0131	0.0524	0.0397	1.0029	0.0053
0.0088	0.0171	0.0150	0.0083	0.0023	0.0047	1.0631
0.0001	0.0003	0.0003	0.0006	0.0010	0.0087	0.0002
0.0114	0.0803	0.1647	0.0286	0.0776	0.0114	0.0323
0.0126	0.0083	0.0055	0.0029	0.0010	0.0008	0.0081
0.0000	0.0000	0.0000	0.0000	0.0000	0.0006	0.0000
0.0017	0.0080	0.0011	0.0013	0.0000	0.0000	0.0004
0.0020	0.0064	0.0069	0.0057	0.0256	0.0154	0.0049
0.0056	0.0005	0.0004	0.0007	0.0006	0.0007	0.0003
0.0000	0.0000	0.0000	0.0000	0.0007	0.0000	0.0000
0.0045	0.0282	0.0277	0.0065	0.0177	0.0270	0.0079

TABLE B-3—*Continued*

Producing sector	Purchasing sector	Tramway and bus transp.	Other road transp.	Water transport
		31	32	33
Agriculture	1	0.0151	0.0010	0.0006
Hunting and fishing	2	0.0000	0.0000	0.0000
Forestry	3	0.0063	0.0039	0.0034
Mining and quarrying	4	0.0022	0.0016	0.0007
Food manufacturing industries	5	0.0002	0.0000	0.0002
Beverage industries	6	0.0000	0.0000	0.0000
Tobacco manufactures	7	0.0000	0.0000	0.0000
Manufacture of textiles	8	0.0024	0.0024	0.0053
Manufacture of footwear, other wearing apparel, and made-up textile goods	9	0.0000	0.0000	0.0019
Manufacture of wood and cork, except manufacture of furniture	10	0.0055	0.0030	0.0018
Manufacture of furniture and fixtures	11	0.0005	0.0003	0.0001
Manufacture of paper and paper products	12	0.0067	0.0047	0.0019
Printing, publishing, and allied industries	13	0.0107	0.0028	0.0019
Manufacture of leather and leather products, except footwear	14	0.0003	0.0002	0.0003
Manufacture of rubber products	15	0.0162	0.0193	0.0004
Manufacture of chemicals and chemical products	16	0.0048	0.0036	0.0037
Manufacture of products of petroleum and asphalt	17	0.0045	0.0041	0.0001
Manufacture of nonmetallic mineral products	18	0.0017	0.0009	0.0012
Basic metal industries	19	0.0224	0.0171	0.0068
Manufacture of metal products, except machinery and transport equipment	20	0.0089	0.0067	0.0028
Manufacture of machinery, except electrical machinery	21	0.0154	0.0117	0.0054
Manufacture of electrical machinery, apparatus, appliances, and supplies	22	0.0122	0.0094	0.0040
Manufacture of transport equipment	23	0.1808	0.1401	0.0487
Miscellaneous industries	24	0.0003	0.0002	0.0002
House construction	25	0.0105	0.0040	0.0019
Other construction and work	26	0.0023	0.0015	0.0109
Electricity, gas, steam and water services	27	0.0353	0.0073	0.0042
Trade	28	0.0351	0.0517	0.0037
Banking and insurance	29	0.0297	0.0163	0.0254
Railway transport	30	0.0094	0.0104	0.0049
Tramway and bus transport	31	1.0004	0.0002	0.0005
Other road transport	32	0.0245	1.0282	0.0073
Water transport	33	0.0100	0.0058	1.0312
Air transport	34	0.0000	0.0000	0.0000
Services incidental to transport	35	0.0004	0.0003	0.0004
Communication	36	0.0053	0.0035	0.0117
Central government	37	0.0003	0.0002	0.0032
Local authorities	38	0.0000	0.0000	0.0000
Other services	39	0.0063	0.0021	0.0030

Air transport	Services incidental to transp.	Communication	Central government	Local authorities	Other services
34	35	36	37	38	39
0.0014	0.0030	0.0018	0.0156	0.0628	0.0070
0.0000	0.0000	0.0000	0.0000	0.0000	0.0000
0.0072	0.0244	0.0117	0.0214	0.0290	0.0576
0.0027	0.0008	0.0025	0.0031	0.0026	0.0053
0.0006	0.0002	0.0002	0.0192	0.0455	0.0005
0.0000	0.0000	0.0000	0.0018	0.0034	0.0000
0.0000	0.0000	0.0000	0.0000	0.0000	0.0000
0.0015	0.0005	0.0004	0.0038	0.0085	0.0003
0.0000	0.0000	0.0000	0.0033	0.0101	0.0000
0.0056	0.0020	0.0070	0.0131	0.0120	0.0135
0.0006	0.0004	0.0012	0.0083	0.0090	0.0017
0.0061	0.0102	0.0055	0.0149	0.0191	0.0161
0.0108	0.0221	0.0079	0.0154	0.0292	0.0164
0.0005	0.0000	0.0000	0.0007	0.0016	0.0000
0.0016	0.0014	0.0009	0.0015	0.0019	0.0004
0.0060	0.0019	0.0044	0.0107	0.0091	0.0067
0.0003	0.0004	0.0007	0.0014	0.0007	0.0006
0.0015	0.0014	0.0075	0.0128	0.0129	0.0077
0.0335	0.0037	0.0182	0.0139	0.0133	0.0053
0.0130	0.0016	0.0058	0.0094	0.0093	0.0034
0.0231	0.0026	0.0120	0.0117	0.0128	0.0032
0.0186	0.0026	0.0365	0.0083	0.0106	0.0029
0.2735	0.0214	0.0116	0.0129	0.0101	0.0034
0.0005	0.0002	0.0059	0.0047	0.0048	0.0016
0.0045	0.0080	0.0238	0.0311	0.0445	0.0723
0.0049	0.0067	0.0586	0.0922	0.0461	0.0030
0.0116	0.0103	0.0311	0.0285	0.0438	0.0577
0.0111	0.0207	0.0114	0.0237	0.0528	0.0238
0.0209	0.0192	0.0125	0.0098	0.0278	0.0568
0.0153	0.0511	0.0239	0.0094	0.0039	0.0056
0.0007	0.0008	0.0282	0.0006	0.0005	0.0007
0.0252	0.0730	0.0206	0.0310	0.0319	0.0131
0.0058	0.0309	0.0031	0.0020	0.0025	0.0029
1.0002	0.0145	0.0006	0.0000	0.0000	0.0000
0.0115	1.0003	0.0002	0.0002	0.0003	0.0003
0.0194	0.0225	1.0175	0.0199	0.0109	0.0074
0.0222	0.0005	0.0007	1.0002	0.0075	0.0004
0.0000	0.0000	0.0000	0.0000	1.0001	0.0000
0.0083	0.0168	0.0106	0.0112	0.0142	1.0215

TABLE B-4

COEFFICIENTS OF PRODUCTION

Adjusted for 1952

Producing sector	Purchasing sector	Agri-culture	Hunting and fishing	Forestry
		1	2	3
Agriculture	1	0.3543	—	0.0711
Hunting and fishing	2	0.0006	—	—
Forestry	3	0.0089	—	—
Mining and quarrying	4	0.0002	—	—
Food manufacturing industries	5	0.0511	—	—
Beverage industries	6	—	—	—
Tobacco manufactures	7	—	—	—
Manufacture of textiles	8	—	—	—
Manufacture of footwear, other wearing apparel, and made-up textile goods	9	—	—	—
Manufacture of wood and cork, except manufacture of furniture	10	—	—	—
Manufacture of furniture and fixtures	11	—	—	—
Manufacture of paper and paper products	12	—	—	—
Printing, publishing, and allied industries	13	—	—	—
Manufacture of leather and leather products, except footwear	14	—	—	—
Manufacture of rubber products	15	—	—	—
Manufacture of chemicals and chemical products	16	0.0257	—	—
Manufacture of products of petroleum and asphalt	17	0.0001	—	—
Manufacture of nonmetallic mineral products	18	0.0001	—	—
Basic metal industries	19	—	—	—
Manufacture of metal products, except machinery and transport equipment	20	0.0017	—	—
Manufacture of machinery, except electrical machinery	21	0.0035	—	0.0049
Manufacture of electrical machinery, apparatus, appliances, and supplies	22	0.0012	—	—
Manufacture of transport equipment	23	0.0034	0.0246	—
Miscellaneous industries	24	0.0005	—	—
House construction	25	0.0114	—	0.0051
Other construction	26	—	—	0.0048
Electricity, gas, steam, and water services	27	0.0058	—	0.0001
Trade	28	0.0207	0.0080	0.0001
Banking and insurance	29	0.0114	—	0.0001
Railway transport	30	0.0048	—	0.0001
Tramway and bus transport	31	—	—	—
Other road transport	32	0.0079	—	0.0001
Water transport	33	0.0016	0.0015	0.0008
Air transport	34	—	—	—
Services incidental to transport	35	0.0002	—	—
Communication	36	0.0011	0.0058	0.0012
Central government	37	0.0006	—	0.0006
Local authorities	38	—	—	0.0001
Other services	39	0.0055	—	—
Labor income		0.4118	0.7872	0.6372
Capital revenue and depreciation		0.1223	0.2026	0.7072
Import		0.0244	0.0141	0.0006
Undistributed plus indirect taxes and subsidies		0.0151	—	0.0030

Mining and quarrying	Food manuf. ind.	Beverage industries	Tobacco manu-factures	Manuf. of textiles	Manuf. of footwear, etc.	Manuf. of wood, etc.
4	5	6	7	8	9	10
—	0.4276	0.0741	—	0.0062	—	—
—	0.0004	—	—	—	0.0023	—
0.0035	0.0027	0.0035	—	0.0021	0.0010	0.4841
0.0359	0.0001	0.0010	—	—	—	—
—	0.1902	0.0309	—	—	—	—
—	0.0001	0.1842	—	—	—	—
—	—	—	0.0164	—	—	—
—	—	—	—	0.0961	0.2910	—
—	—	—	—	0.0073	0.0205	—
0.0018	0.0027	0.0145	0.0200	0.0013	0.0023	0.0770
—	—	—	—	—	—	—
0.0154	0.0123	—	0.1719	0.0125	0.0103	0.0036
0.0017	0.0042	0.0197	0.0710	0.0061	0.0054	0.0022
—	—	—	—	—	0.0888	—
—	—	—	—	0.0025	0.0111	—
0.1219	0.0079	0.0212	0.0020	0.0384	0.0026	0.0074
—	—	—	—	0.0023	—	0.0004
—	—	0.0987	—	—	—	0.0003
—	—	—	—	—	—	—
—	0.0047	0.0098	—	—	0.0074	0.0024
0.0384	0.0005	0.0017	—	—	—	0.0064
0.0282	—	—	—	—	—	—
—	0.0003	—	—	—	—	—
—	0.0005	—	0.0067	0.0019	0.0042	—
0.0105	0.0042	0.0077	0.0023	0.0067	0.0027	0.0070
0.0114	—	—	—	—	—	—
0.0559	0.0075	0.0192	0.0047	0.0186	0.0051	0.0343
0.0081	0.0128	0.0072	0.0044	0.0089	0.0135	0.0015
0.0097	0.0066	0.0086	0.0060	0.0107	0.0102	0.0226
0.0008	0.0041	0.0068	0.0063	0.0082	0.0088	0.0099
—	—	—	—	—	—	—
0.0243	0.0169	0.0410	0.0067	0.0079	0.0073	0.0342
0.0032	0.0072	0.0058	0.0200	0.0195	0.0050	0.0041
—	—	—	—	—	—	—
—	0.0006	0.0009	0.0023	0.0023	0.0005	0.0002
0.0043	0.0009	0.0023	0.0027	0.0058	0.0048	0.0031
0.0054	0.0005	0.0019	—	0.0002	0.0002	0.0003
—	0.0007	0.0012	—	—	—	—
0.0018	0.0029	0.0082	0.0668	0.0071	0.0038	0.0014
0.3471	0.0966	0.1935	0.2217	0.4381	0.4220	0.3150
0.2126	0.0462	0.0915	0.0759	0.2047	0.1083	0.0073
0.0284	0.1017	0.0807	0.3183	0.2910	0.0793	0.0182
0.0522	0.0243	0.1340	0.0758	0.1120	0.0676	0.0068

TABLE B-4—*Continued*

Producing sector	Purchasing sector	Manuf. of furniture, etc.	Manuf. of paper, etc.	Printing publishing etc.
		11	12	13
Agriculture	1	—	—	—
Hunting and fishing	2	—	—	—
Forestry	3	0.0010	0.1863	0.0006
Mining and quarrying	4	—	0.0098	—
Food manufacturing industries	5	—	—	—
Beverage industries	6	—	—	—
Tobacco manufactures	7	—	—	—
Manufacture of textiles	8	0.0170	0.0002	0.0024
Manufacture of footwear, other wearing apparel, and made-up textile goods	9	—	—	—
Manufacture of wood and cork, except manufacture of furniture	10	0.1403	0.0121	—
Manufacture of furniture and fixtures	11	0.0227	—	—
Manufacture of paper and paper products	12	0.0084	0.2757	0.1614
Printing, publishing, and allied industries	13	0.0089	0.0018	0.2964
Manufacture of leather and leather products, except footwear	14	—	—	0.0006
Manufacture of rubber products	15	0.0004	—	—
Manufacture of chemicals and chemical products	16	0.0177	0.0244	0.0087
Manufacture of products of petroleum and asphalt	17	—	0.0002	—
Manufacture of nonmetallic mineral products	18	—	—	—
Basic metal industries	19	0.0018	—	—
Manufacture of metal products, except machinery and transport equipment	20	0.0183	0.0005	—
Manufacture of machinery, except electrical machinery	21	0.0014	0.0089	0.0003
Manufacture of electrical machinery, apparatus, appliances, and supplies	22	—	0.0033	—
Manufacture of transport equipment	23	—	—	—
Miscellaneous industries	24	—	—	—
House construction	25	0.0050	0.0066	0.0055
Other construction	26	—	—	—
Electricity, gas, steam, and water services	27	0.0138	0.1136	0.0070
Trade	28	0.0036	0.0015	0.0041
Banking and insurance	29	0.0197	0.0256	0.0071
Railway transport	30	0.0037	0.0092	0.0031
Tramway and bus transport	31	—	—	—
Other road transport	32	0.0055	0.0213	0.0075
Water transport	33	0.0016	0.0044	0.0010
Air transport	34	—	—	—
Services incidental to transport	35	—	0.0002	—
Communication	36	0.0022	0.0018	0.0045
Central government	37	0.0004	0.0003	0.0003
Local authorities	38	—	—	—
Other services	39	0.0015	0.0015	0.0153
Labor income		0.2646	0.1824	0.4522
Capital revenue and depreciation		0.0745	0.1667	0.1616
Import		0.0265	0.0198	0.0092
Undustributed plus indirect taxes and subsidies		0.0139	0.0240	0.0394

Manuf. of leather, etc.	Manuf. of rubber products	Manuf. of chemicals, etc.	Manuf. of petroleum, etc.	Manuf. of nonmet. mineral pr.	Basic metal ind.	Manuf. of metal pr., etc.
14	15	16	17	18	19	20
—	—	0.0117	—	—	—	—
—	—	—	—	—	—	—
0.0036	0.0010	0.0019	—	0.0113	0.0008	0.0026
—	—	0.0103	0.0652	0.0645	0.0756	—
0.1268	—	0.0058	—	—	—	—
—	—	0.0030	—	—	—	—
—	—	—	—	—	—	—
0.0135	0.0644	0.0008	—	—	—	0.0028
—	—	—	—	—	—	—
—	0.0022	0.0014	—	0.0091	0.0005	0.0054
—	—	—	—	—	—	—
0.0624	0.0129	0.0576	0.1197	0.0214	0.0011	0.0099
0.0035	0.0061	0.0131	—	0.0054	0.0010	0.0036
0.0522	—	—	—	—	—	0.0010
0.0019	0.0571	—	—	—	—	0.0016
0.0158	0.0121	0.1327	0.0179	0.0250	0.0168	0.0168
—	—	0.0002	0.0145	0.0004	0.0003	0.0004
—	—	0.0164	—	0.0589	—	0.0011
—	—	0.0002	—	0.0114	0.4769	0.1140
—	0.0011	0.0213	—	0.0029	0.0166	0.0603
0.0089	—	0.0025	—	0.0007	0.0030	0.0011
—	—	0.0013	—	—	0.0024	0.0214
—	—	0.0026	—	—	0.0006	—
—	—	0.0009	—	—	—	0.0004
0.0058	0.0080	0.0074	0.0055	0.0153	0.0051	0.0040
—	—	—	—	—	—	—
0.0116	0.0226	0.0420	0.0110	0.0370	0.0254	0.0197
0.0127	0.0075	0.0105	0.0103	0.0137	0.0058	0.0091
0.0174	0.0146	0.0088	0.0141	0.0156	0.0069	0.0082
0.0086	0.0050	0.0068	0.0778	0.0227	0.0094	0.0057
—	—	—	—	—	—	—
0.0165	0.0085	0.0089	0.0104	0.1055	0.0034	0.0156
0.0165	0.0116	0.0184	0.0233	0.0069	0.0081	0.0131
—	—	0.0006	—	—	—	—
0.0019	0.0011	0.0020	0.0052	0.0007	0.0008	0.0011
0.0044	0.0039	0.0064	—	0.0035	0.0030	0.0041
—	—	—	—	0.0004	0.0005	0.0011
—	—	—	—	—	—	0.0005
0.0037	0.0032	0.0037	0.0052	0.0024	0.0025	0.0015
0.3761	0.3055	0.1996	0.1767	0.4118	0.1349	0.4223
0.1933	0.3327	0.2230	0.0972	0.1755	0.0806	0.1599
0.2410	0.1960	0.2753	0.3417	0.0768	0.1045	0.1830
0.0734	0.0550	0.1331	0.1041	0.0237	0.0740	0.0439

TABLE B-4—*Continued*

Producing sector	Purchasing sector	Manuf. of machinery, etc.	Manuf. of elec. mach., etc.	Manuf. of transport equipm.
		21	22	23
Agriculture	1	—	—	—
Hunting and fishing	2	—	—	—
Forestry	3	0.0025	—	0.0034
Mining and quarrying	4	—	—	—
Food manufacturing industries	5	—	—	—
Beverage industries	6	—	—	—
Tobacco manufactures	7	—	—	—
Manufacture of textiles	8	0.0003	0.0006	0.0026
Manufacture of footwear, other wearing apparel, and made-up textile goods	9	—	—	—
Manufacture of wood and cork, except manufacture of furniture	10	0.0073	0.0008	0.0111
Manufacture of furniture and fixtures	11	0.0016	0.0150	—
Manufacture of paper and paper products	12	0.0047	0.0082	0.0036
Printing, publishing, and allied industries	13	0.0029	0.0069	0.0019
Manufacture of leather and leather products, except footwear	14	0.0014	—	0.0010
Manufacture of rubber products	15	0.0026	—	0.0032
Manufacture of chemicals and chemical products	16	0.0185	0.0059	0.0062
Manufacture of products of petroleum and asphalt	17	0.0005	0.0002	0.0003
Manufacture of nonmetallic mineral products	18	0.0021	0.0072	0.0008
Basic metal industries	19	0.0955	0.0909	0.0330
Manufacture of metal products, except machinery and transport equipment	20	0.0356	0.0221	0.0295
Manufacture of machinery, except electrical machinery	21	0.0499	0.0094	0.0623
Manufacture of electrical machinery, apparatus, appliances, and supplies	22	0.0758	0.0670	0.0778
Manufacture of transport equipment	23	—	—	0.0145
Miscellaneous industries	24	0.0007	—	0.0008
House construction	25	0.0050	0.0018	0.0030
Other construction	26	—	—	—
Electricity, gas, steam, and water services	27	0.0173	0.0081	0.0096
Trade	28	0.0080	0.0058	0.0051
Banking and insurance	29	0.0063	0.0042	0.0061
Railway transport	30	0.0062	0.0040	0.0029
Tramway and bus transport	31	—	—	—
Other road transport	32	0.0129	0.0043	0.0105
Water transport	33	0.0102	0.0064	0.0108
Air transport	34	0.0004	—	—
Services incidental to transport	35	0.0009	0.0008	0.0011
Communication	36	0.0046	0.0022	0.0029
Central government	37	0.0011	0.0008	0.0005
Local authorities	38	0.0003	0.0003	0.0002
Other services	39	0.0026	0.0020	0.0023
Labor income		0.4491	0.2043	0.3795
Capital revenue and depreciation		0.1555	0.1121	0.1241
Import		0.1374	0.0940	0.1446
Undistributed plus indirect taxes and subsidies		0.0612	0.0172	0.0199

Misc. manuf. ind.	House con- struction	Other con- struction	Elec- tricity, etc.	Trade	Banking and insurance	Railway trans- port
24	25	26	27	28	29	30
—	0.0083	—	—	—	—	0.0048
—	—	—	—	—	—	—
0.0013	0.0049	0.0076	0.0128	—	—	0.0583
0.0146	0.0038	0.0051	0.0025	—	—	0.0050
—	—	—	0.0004	—	—	—
—	—	—	—	—	—	—
—	—	—	—	—	—	—
0.0021	0.0002	—	0.0009	—	—	—
—	—	—	0.0001	—	—	—
0.0268	0.0405	0.0488	0.0436	—	—	—
—	0.0347	—	—	—	—	0.0047
0.0090	0.0070	0.0144	0.0024	0.0179	0.0032	0.0004
0.0060	—	—	0.0018	0.0194	0.0032	0.0018
0.0011	—	—	0.0002	—	—	—
0.0013	0.0015	—	—	—	—	—
0.0276	0.0081	0.0119	0.0046	—	—	0.0018
—	0.0054	0.0047	0.0001	—	—	0.0007
0.0039	0.0914	0.0701	0.0008	—	—	—
0.0567	0.0158	0.0135	0.0003	—	—	—
0.0075	0.0315	0.0215	0.0001	—	—	—
0.0099	0.0147	0.0111	0.0025	0.0003	—	—
0.0022	0.0173	0.0515	0.0010	0.0017	—	—
—	0.0090	0.0108	0.0008	—	—	0.1444
0.0254	0.0010	0.0045	—	—	—	—
0.0054	—	—	0.0104	0.0109	0.0104	0.0499
—	—	—	0.0291	—	—	0.1041
0.0161	0.0039	0.0007	0.3880	0.0030	0.0026	0.0083
0.0140	0.0412	0.0273	0.0079	0.0335	0.0041	0.0078
0.0052	0.0056	0.0041	0.0377	0.0471	—	0.0006
0.0048	0.0084	0.0065	0.0027	—	0.0024	0.0560
—	—	—	—	—	0.0061	—
0.0038	0.0541	0.1352	0.0075	0.0706	0.0061	0.0083
0.0081	0.0032	0.0006	0.0006	—	0.0002	0.0039
—	—	—	—	—	0.0004	—
0.0013	0.0004	0.0007	0.0007	—	—	—
—	0.0034	0.0043	0.0024	0.0279	0.0128	0.0033
0.0051	0.0001	—	0.0003	0.0005	0.0004	—
—	—	—	—	0.0009	—	—
0.0025	0.0236	0.0234	0.0014	0.0147	0.0190	0.0028
0.5130	0.4432	0.4819	0.1337	0.6054	0.2874	0.7195
0.1656	0.0447	0.0565	0.3089	0.4507	0.5413	0.0540
0.1235	0.0377	0.0167	0.0853	—	0.1014	0.0675
0.0832	0.0944	0.0387	0.0284	0.0140	0.0005	−0.0714

TABLE B-4—*Continued*

Producing sector	Purchasing sector	Tramway and bus transp.	Other road transp.	Water trans-port
		31	32	33
Agriculture	1	—	—	—
Hunting and fishing	2	—	—	—
Forestry	3	—	—	0.0012
Mining and quarrying	4	—	—	—
Food manufacturing industries	5	—	—	—
Beverage industries	6	—	—	—
Tobacco manufactures	7	—	—	—
Manufacture of textiles	8	—	—	0.0035
Manufacture of footwear, other wearing apparel, and made-up textile goods	9	—	—	0.0017
Manufacture of wood and cork, except manufacture of furniture	10	—	—	—
Manufacture of furniture and fixtures	11	—	—	—
Manufacture of paper and paper products	12	—	0.0001	—
Printing, publishing, and allied industries	13	0.0052	—	0.0006
Manufacture of leather and leather products, except footwear	14	—	—	—
Manufacture of rubber products	15	0.0144	0.0174	—
Manufacture of chemicals and chemical products	16	—	—	0.0016
Manufacture of products of petroleum and asphalt	17	0.0039	0.0035	—
Manufacture of nonmetallic mineral products	18	—	—	—
Basic metal industries	19	—	—	—
Manufacture of metal products, except machinery and transport equipment	20	—	—	—
Manufacture of machinery, except electrical machinery	21	—	—	0.0010
Manufacture of electrical machinery, apparatus, appliances, and supplies	22	—	—	—
Manufacture of transport equipment	23	0.2040	0.1565	0.0587
Miscellaneous industries	24	—	—	—
House construction	25	0.0075	0.0015	0.0004
Other construction	26	—	—	0.0107
Electricity, gas, steam, and water services	27	0.0170	0.0003	0.0007
Trade	28	0.0293	0.0462	0.0019
Banking and insurance	29	0.0332	0.0165	0.0351
Railway transport	30	0.0059	0.0074	0.0034
Tramway and bus transport	31	—	—	—
Other road transport	32	0.0162	0.0205	0.0037
Water transport	33	0.0051	0.0022	0.0290
Air transport	34	—	—	—
Services incidental to transport	35	—	—	0.0042
Communication	36	0.0033	0.0014	0.0135
Central government	37	—	—	0.0033
Local authorities	38	—	—	—
Other services	39	0.0035	—	0.0016
Labor income		0.4229	0.5463	0.4104
Capital revenue and depreciation		0.2706	0.1822	0.4658
Import		0.0580	0.0406	0.2926
Undistributed plus indirect taxes and subsidies		0.1169	0.1498	0.0056

Air transport	Services incidental to transp.	Communication	Central government	Local authorities	Other services
34	35	36	37	38	39
—	—	—	—	0.0157	—
—	—	—	—	—	—
—	0.0168	0.0033	0.0088	0.0121	0.0438
—	—	—	0.0003	—	0.0041
—	—	—	0.0160	0.0281	—
—	—	—	0.0014	0.0021	—
—	—	—	—	—	—
—	—	—	0.0015	0.0024	—
—	—	—	0.0028	0.0065	—
—	—	—	0.0018	0.0012	0.0056
—	—	—	0.0123	0.0099	—
—	0.0029	—	0.0043	0.0037	0.0068
0.0052	0.0135	0.0032	0.0086	0.0129	0.0095
—	—	—	0.0003	0.0003	—
—	—	—	0.0007	0.0008	—
—	—	—	0.0031	0.0003	0.0019
—	—	—	0.0005	—	—
—	—	—	0.0019	0.0031	—
—	—	—	0.0010	0.0006	—
—	—	0.0005	0.0034	0.0028	—
—	—	0.0066	0.0072	0.0065	0.0004
—	—	0.0412	0.0036	0.0076	0.0016
0.3107	—	—	0.0072	0.0035	—
—	—	0.0044	0.0039	0.0032	0.0014
—	0.0031	0.0176	0.0291	0.0321	0.0719
—	—	0.0482	0.0945	0.0350	—
—	0.0031	0.0129	0.0123	0.0160	0.0320
0.0054	0.0144	0.0038	0.0149	0.0320	0.0170
0.0223	0.0196	0.0093	0.0065	0.0212	0.0694
0.0103	0.0432	0.0156	0.0051	—	0.0028
—	—	0.0231	—	—	—
0.0165	0.0664	0.0054	0.0094	0.0098	0.0032
—	0.0260	0.0009	—	—	0.0015
—	0.0145	0.0005	—	—	—
0.0110	—	—	—	—	0.0002
0.0197	0.0241	0.0158	0.0211	0.0071	0.0061
0.0219	—	0.0004	—	0.0055	0.0002
—	—	—	—	—	—
0.0055	0.0145	0.0059	0.0064	0.0067	0.0169
0.3199	0.5365	0.6218	0.7157	0.4755	0.3698
0.2149	0.4765	0.1541	0.0610	0.1090	0.6700
0.1877	0.0127	0.0176	0.0583	0.0142	0.0111
0.0220	0.0029	0.0187	0.0363	0.0283	0.0151

TABLE B-5

Inverse of the Identity Matrix Less the Matrix of Coefficients of Production

Adjusted for 1952

Producing sector	Purchasing sector	Agri-culture	Hunting and fishing	Forestry
		1	2	3
Agriculture	1	0.0162	0.0001	0.1154
Hunting and fishing	2	0.0009	1.0000	0.0001
Forestry	3	0.0196	0.0005	1.0019
Mining and quarrying	4	0.0019	0.0002	0.0004
Food manufacturing industries	5	0.1027	0.0000	0.0073
Beverage industries	6	0.0002	0.0000	0.0000
Tobacco manufactures	7	0.0000	0.0000	0.0000
Manufacture of textiles	8	0.0002	0.0001	0.0000
Manufacture of footwear, other wearing apparel, and made-up textile goods	9	0.0000	0.0000	0.0000
Manufacture of wood and cork, except manufacture of furniture	10	0.0033	0.0004	0.0009
Manufacture of furniture and fixtures	11	0.0009	0.0001	0.0003
Manufacture of paper and paper products	12	0.0086	0.0006	0.0010
Printing, publishing, and allied industries	13	0.0033	0.0004	0.0003
Manufacture of leather and leather products, except footwear	14	0.0000	0.0000	0.0000
Manufacture of rubber products	15	0.0005	0.0001	0.0001
Manufacture of chemicals and chemical products	16	0.0506	0.0004	0.0040
Manufacture of products of petroleum and asphalt	17	0.0004	0.0000	0.0001
Manufacture of nonmetallic mineral products	18	0.0035	0.0001	0.0012
Basic metal industries	19	0.0053	0.0026	0.0020
Manufacture of metal products, except machinery and transport equipment	20	0.0063	0.0010	0.0010
Manufacture of machinery, except electrical machiner	21	0.0078	0.0018	0.0059
Manufacture of electrical machinery, apparatus, appliances, and supplies	22	0.0048	0.0026	0.0013
Manufacture of transport equipment	23	0.0113	0.0254	0.0013
Miscellaneous industries	24	0.0009	0.0001	0.0001
House construction	25	0.0221	0.0004	0.0069
Other construction and work	26	0.0023	0.0004	0.0051
Electricity, gas, steam, and water services	27	0.0247	0.0010	0.0025
Trade	28	0.0397	0.0086	0.0035
Banking and insurance	29	0.0246	0.0009	0.0022
Railway transport	30	0.0101	0.0003	0.0011
Tramway and bus transport	31	0.0002	0.0002	0.0001
Other road transport	32	0.0214	0.0011	0.0029
Water transport	33	0.0050	0.0019	0.0014
Air transport	34	0.0001	0.0000	0.0000
Services incidental to transport	35	0.0006	0.0000	0.0001
Communication	36	0.0043	0.0063	0.0017
Central government	37	0.0012	0.0000	0.0007
Local authorities	38	0.0001	0.0000	0.0001
Other services	39	0.0114	0.0003	0.0011

Mining and quarrying	Food manuf. ind.	Beverage industries	Tobacco manu- factures	Manuf. of textiles	Manuf. of footwear, etc.	Manuf. of wood, etc.
4	5	6	7	8	9	10
0.0063	0.8575	0.1838	0.0087	0.0141	0.0161	0.0617
0.0000	0.0010	0.0001	0.0000	0.0000	0.0023	0.0000
0.0189	0.0221	0.0263	0.0698	0.0122	0.0138	0.5310
1.0416	0.0020	0.0121	0.0040	0.0017	0.0014	0.0012
0.0017	1.2894	0.0589	0.0007	0.0014	0.0162	0.0041
0.0006	0.0003	1.2260	0.0000	0.0002	0.0001	0.0000
0.0000	0.0000	0.0000	1.0167	0.0000	0.0000	0.0000
0.0005	0.0003	0.0005	0.0006	1.1095	0.3321	0.0002
0.0000	0.0000	0.0000	0.0001	0.0083	1.0234	0.0000
0.0107	0.0074	0.0256	0.0304	0.0052	0.0062	1.0880
0.0013	0.0008	0.0009	0.0006	0.0005	0.0004	0.0006
0.0384	0.0295	0.0191	0.2679	0.0276	0.0354	0.0088
0.0073	0.0103	0.0381	0.1054	0.0117	0.0132	0.0044
0.0001	0.0001	0.0001	0.0001	0.0008	0.0959	0.0001
0.0009	0.0008	0.0015	0.0004	0.0033	0.0135	0.0009
0.1510	0.0396	0.0442	0.0133	0.0516	0.0227	0.0128
0.0004	0.0004	0.0005	0.0002	0.0027	0.0009	0.0007
0.0060	0.0030	0.1317	0.0019	0.0023	0.0016	0.0025
0.0182	0.0057	0.0100	0.0034	0.0022	0.0043	0.0050
0.0077	0.0104	0.0167	0.0016	0.0021	0.0096	0.0047
0.0448	0.0059	0.0059	0.0044	0.0015	0.0024	0.0117
0.0380	0.0039	0.0040	0.0030	0.0018	0.0020	0.0030
0.0078	0.0121	0.0161	0.0064	0.0058	0.0063	0.0097
0.0003	0.0012	0.0003	0.0071	0.0024	0.0052	0.0001
0.0158	0.0188	0.0185	0.0126	0.0108	0.0091	0.0136
0.0169	0.0029	0.0044	0.0041	0.0033	0.0033	0.0063
0.1176	0.0355	0.0615	0.0670	0.0451	0.0322	0.0664
0.0157	0.0398	0.0226	0.0099	0.0137	0.0221	0.0073
0.0203	0.0253	0.0237	0.0243	0.0181	0.0216	0.0303
0.0046	0.0118	0.0158	0.0115	0.0117	0.0151	0.0133
0.0003	0.0003	0.0003	0.0003	0.0003	0.0003	0.0003
0.0358	0.0365	0.0752	0.0187	0.0140	0.0176	0.0428
0.0080	0.0127	0.0111	0.0234	0.0241	0.0151	0.0061
0.0001	0.0001	0.0001	0.0001	0.0001	0.0001	0.0000
0.0006	0.0012	0.0015	0.0026	0.0029	0.0016	0.0004
0.0076	0.0047	0.0061	0.0059	0.0085	0.0094	0.0055
0.0059	0.0014	0.0028	0.0004	0.0005	0.0005	0.0008
0.0000	0.0010	0.0015	0.0000	0.0000	0.0000	0.0001
0.0047	0.0108	0.0143	0.0727	0.0097	0.0086	0.0035

TABLE B-5—*Continued*

Producing sector	Purchasing sector	Manuf. of furniture, etc.	Manuf. of paper, etc.	Printing, publishing, etc.
		11	12	13
Agriculture	1	0.0106	0.0338	0.0089
Hunting and fishing	2	0.0000	0.0000	0.0000
Forestry	3	0.0830	0.2799	0.0682
Mining and quarrying	4	0.0016	0.0164	0.0044
Food manufacturing industries	5	0.0009	0.0026	0.0010
Beverage industries	6	0.0001	0.0002	0.0001
Tobacco manufactures	7	0.0000	0.0000	0.0000
Manufacture of textiles	8	0.0196	0.0009	0.0042
Manufacture of footwear, other wearing apparel, and made-up textile goods	9	0.0002	0.0000	0.0000
Manufacture of wood and cork, except manufacture of furniture	10	0.1586	0.0327	0.0093
Manufacture of furniture and fixtures	11	1.0236	0.0009	0.0006
Manufacture of paper and paper products	12	0.0195	1.3886	0.3210
Printing, publishing, and allied industries	13	0.0149	0.0061	1.4238
Manufacture of leather and leather products, except footwear	14	0.0001	0.0001	0.0010
Manufacture of rubber products	15	0.0008	0.0009	0.0005
Manufacture of chemicals and chemical products	16	0.0255	0.0455	0.0255
Manufacture of products of petroleum and asphalt	17	0.0003	0.0006	0.0003
Manufacture of nonmetallic mineral products	18	0.0017	0.0037	0.0023
Basic metal industries	19	0.0099	0.0074	0.0029
Manufacture of metal products, except machinery and transport equipment	20	0.0219	0.0041	0.0019
Manufacture of machinery, except electrical machinery	21	0.0040	0.0175	0.0052
Manufacture of electrical machinery, apparatus, appliances, and supplies	22	0.0019	0.0094	0.0033
Manufacture of transport equipment	23	0.0040	0.0100	0.0056
Miscellaneous industries	24	0.0001	0.0002	0.0002
House construction	25	0.0091	0.0168	0.0145
Other construction and work	26	0.0027	0.0115	0.0042
Electricity, gas, steam, and water services	27	0.0405	0.2673	0.0812
Trade	28	0.0071	0.0097	0.0105
Banking and insurance	29	0.0279	0.0499	0.0251
Railway transport	30	0.0072	0.0164	0.0092
Tramway and bus transport	31	0.0003	0.0004	0.0004
Other road transport	32	0.0151	0.0393	0.0223
Water transport	33	0.0041	0.0087	0.0041
Air transport	34	0.0000	0.0001	0.0000
Services incidental to transport	35	0.0002	0.0007	0.0002
Communication	36	0.0043	0.0056	0.0086
Central government	37	0.0006	0.0009	0.0007
Local authorities	38	0.0000	0.0001	0.0000
Other services	39	0.0035	0.0051	0.0241

Manuf. of leather, etc.	Manuf. of rubber products	Manuf. of chemicals, etc.	Manuf. of petroleum, etc.	Manuf. of nonmet. mineral pr.	Basic metal ind.	Manuf. of metal pr., etc.
14	15	16	17	18	19	20
0.1187	0.0027	0.0321	0.0068	0.0054	0.0034	0.0027
0.0001	0.0000	0.0000	0.0000	0.0000	0.0000	0.0000
0.0286	0.0104	0.0291	0.0432	0.0319	0.0124	0.0137
0.0022	0.0010	0.0163	0.0722	0.0752	0.1526	0.0199
0.1730	0.0004	0.0107	0.0008	0.0007	0.0008	0.0007
0.0001	0.0001	0.0043	0.0001	0.0002	0.0002	0.0001
0.0000	0.0000	0.0000	0.0000	0.0000	0.0000	0.0000
0.0163	0.0760	0.0015	0.0004	0.0005	0.0005	0.0037
0.0002	0.0006	0.0001	0.0001	0.0000	0.0001	0.0001
0.0052	0.0061	0.0098	0.0073	0.0173	0.0084	0.0102
0.0006	0.0005	0.0006	0.0010	0.0011	0.0009	0.0008
0.1000	0.0252	0.1009	0.1747	0.0413	0.0149	0.0212
0.0085	0.0110	0.0238	0.0028	0.0110	0.0061	0.0078
1.0551	0.0001	0.0001	0.0001	0.0001	0.0001	0.0011
0.0028	1.0611	0.0005	0.0006	0.0025	0.0005	0.0023
0.0294	0.0200	1.1623	0.0379	0.0450	0.0617	0.0302
0.0003	0.0003	0.0005	1.0151	0.0011	0.0008	0.0007
0.0021	0.0017	0.0227	0.0032	1.0662	0.0035	0.0032
0.0047	0.0018	0.0107	0.0050	0.0297	1.9262	0.2399
0.0032	0.0024	0.0281	0.0029	0.0071	0.0374	1.0706
0.0127	0.0012	0.0065	0.0069	0.0071	0.0141	0.0043
0.0033	0.0014	0.0058	0.0063	0.0067	0.0136	0.0276
0.0087	0.0045	0.0104	0.0187	0.0253	0.0089	0.0068
0.0003	0.0002	0.0012	0.0002	0.0002	0.0002	0.0006
0.0120	0.0113	0.0136	0.0145	0.0222	0.0159	0.0085
0.0036	0.0028	0.0054	0.0125	0.0071	0.0079	0.0037
0.0471	0.0493	0.1058	0.0636	0.0869	0.1048	0.0548
0.0226	0.0114	0.0179	0.0164	0.0253	0.0176	0.0149
0.0291	0.0212	0.0214	0.0258	0.0275	0.0231	0.0164
0.0135	0.0076	0.0119	0.0871	0.0291	0.0217	0.0106
0.0004	0.0003	0.0004	0.0002	0.0003	0.0004	0.0003
0.0289	0.0139	0.0217	0.0235	0.1247	0.0177	0.0231
0.0215	0.0151	0.0240	0.0274	0.0104	0.0192	0.0179
0.0001	0.0000	0.0007	0.0001	0.0001	0.0001	0.0001
0.0024	0.0015	0.0026	0.0056	0.0010	0.0019	0.0016
0.0074	0.0060	0.0100	0.0031	0.0068	0.0091	0.0070
0.0004	0.0001	0.0004	0.0006	0.0010	0.0020	0.0016
0.0002	0.0000	0.0001	0.0000	0.0000	0.0000	0.0006
0.0073	0.0055	0.0069	0.0080	0.0054	0.0074	0.0038

TABLE B-5—*Continued*

Producing sector	Purchasing sector	Manuf. of machinery, etc.	Manuf. of elec. mach., etc.	Manuf. of transport equipm.
		21	22	23
Agriculture	1	0.0029	0.0016	0.0024
Hunting and fishing	2	0.0000	0.0000	0.0000
Forestry	3	0.0139	0.0083	0.0146
Mining and quarrying	4	0.0184	0.0167	0.0087
Food manufacturing industries	5	0.0008	0.0003	0.0005
Beverage industries	6	0.0001	0.0001	0.0001
Tobacco manufactures	7	0.0000	0.0000	0.0000
Manufacture of textiles	8	0.0011	0.0014	0.0036
Manufacture of footwear, other wearing apparel, and made-up textile goods	9	0.0000	0.0000	0.0001
Manufacture of wood and cork, except manufacture of furniture	10	0.0129	0.0064	0.0156
Manufacture of furniture and fixtures	11	0.0035	0.0169	0.0018
Manufacture of paper and paper products	12	0.0149	0.0186	0.0108
Printing, publishing, and allied industries	13	0.0075	0.0124	0.0054
Manufacture of leather and leather products, except footwear	14	0.0017	0.0001	0.0012
Manufacture of rubber products	15	0.0035	0.0003	0.0041
Manufacture of chemicals and chemical products	16	0.0325	0.0162	0.0147
Manufacture of products of petroleum and asphalt	17	0.0008	0.0004	0.0006
Manufacture of nonmetallic mineral products	18	0.0050	0.0097	0.0029
Basic metal industries	19	0.2198	0.1968	0.1020
Manufacture of metal products, except machinery and transport equipment	20	0.0475	0.0305	0.0394
Manufacture of machinery, except electrical machinery	21	1.0562	0.0129	0.0691
Manufacture of electrical machinery, apparatus, appliances, and supplies	22	0.0895	1.0755	0.0926
Manufacture of transport equipment	23	0.0065	0.0038	1.0195
Miscellaneous industries	24	0.0009	0.0001	0.0010
House construction	25	0.0100	0.0086	0.0065
Other construction and work	26	0.0036	0.0024	0.0022
Electricity, gas, steam, and water services	27	0.0507	0.0321	0.0305
Trade	28	0.0142	0.0102	0.0097
Banking and insurance	29	0.0145	0.0104	0.0120
Railway transport	30	0.0114	0.0081	0.0064
Tramway and bus transport	31	0.0003	0.0002	0.0002
Other road transport	32	0.0210	0.0107	0.0168
Water transport	33	0.0155	0.0102	0.0149
Air transport	34	0.0005	0.0000	0.0001
Services incidental to transport	35	0.0015	0.0012	0.0015
Communication	36	0.0076	0.0044	0.0052
Central government	37	0.0017	0.0012	0.0009
Local authorities	38	0.0004	0.0004	0.0003
Other services	39	0.0050	0.0039	0.0041

Misc. manuf. ind.	House con- struction	Other con- struction	Elec- tricity, etc.	Trade	Banking and insurance	Railway trans- port
24	25	26	27	28	29	30
0.0041	0.0187	0.0059	0.0087	0.0013	0.0006	0.0177
0.0000	0.0000	0.0000	0.0000	0.0000	0.0000	0.0000
0.0233	0.0388	0.0444	0.0641	0.0088	0.0032	0.0729
0.0262	0.0157	0.0156	0.0060	0.0009	0.0004	0.0096
0.0009	0.0014	0.0006	0.0016	0.0002	0.0001	0.0012
0.0002	0.0001	0.0001	0.0000	0.0000	0.0000	0.0000
0.0000	0.0000	0.0000	0.0000	0.0000	0.0000	0.0000
0.0028	0.0015	0.0006	0.0018	0.0003	0.0001	0.0009
0.0001	0.0000	0.0000	0.0002	0.0000	0.0000	0.0000
0.0334	0.0535	0.0571	0.0817	0.0023	0.0013	0.0133
0.0006	0.0363	0.0013	0.0009	0.0006	0.0005	0.0075
0.0211	0.0203	0.0296	0.0109	0.0335	0.0063	0.0085
0.0111	0.0046	0.0041	0.0059	0.0297	0.0052	0.0048
0.0013	0.0001	0.0001	0.0005	0.0000	0.0000	0.0002
0.0018	0.0033	0.0031	0.0006	0.0015	0.0003	0.0014
0.0412	0.0199	0.0230	0.0126	0.0021	0.0007	0.0097
0.0002	0.0060	0.0055	0.0007	0.0004	0.0001	0.0018
0.0063	0.0988	0.0765	0.0074	0.0017	0.0014	0.0144
0.1183	0.0507	0.0507	0.0067	0.0030	0.0012	0.0245
0.0126	0.0385	0.0283	0.0033	0.0013	0.0007	0.0116
0.0135	0.0195	0.0170	0.0072	0.0022	0.0007	0.0144
0.0059	0.0246	0.0620	0.0067	0.0052	0.0014	0.0231
0.0042	0.0242	0.0382	0.0078	0.0132	0.0035	0.1636
1.0262	0.0012	0.0048	0.0003	0.0002	0.0001	0.0008
0.0095	1.0077	0.0072	0.0205	0.0148	0.0127	0.0565
0.0034	0.0033	1.0030	0.0493	0.0023	0.0013	0.1123
0.0454	0.0301	0.0250	1.6447	0.0148	0.0077	0.0256
0.0187	0.0513	0.0402	0.0185	1.0404	0.0061	0.0186
0.0123	0.0184	0.0167	0.0672	0.0539	1.0029	0.0076
0.0083	0.0151	0.0132	0.0073	0.0022	0.0032	1.0631
0.0001	0.0003	0.0003	0.0006	0.0010	0.0065	0.0002
0.0115	0.0759	0.1556	0.0272	0.0784	0.0084	0.0345
0.0114	0.0071	0.0047	0.0024	0.0009	0.0005	0.0078
0.0001	0.0000	0.0000	0.0001	0.0001	0.0004	0.0000
0.0017	0.0008	0.0010	0.0012	0.0001	0.0000	0.0004
0.0024	0.0072	0.0078	0.0065	0.0309	0.0136	0.0063
0.0056	0.0005	0.0004	0.0007	0.0006	0.0005	0.0003
0.0000	0.0001	0.0001	0.0000	0.0010	0.0000	0.0001
0.0046	0.0267	0.0262	0.0062	0.0179	0.0200	0.0084

TABLE B-5—*Continued*

Producing sector	Purchasing sector	Tramway and bus transp.	Other road transp.	Water transport
		31	32	33
Agriculture	1	0.0011	0.0007	0.0007
Hunting and fishing	2	0.0000	0.0000	0.0000
Forestry	3	0.0061	0.0038	0.0036
Mining and quarrying	4	0.0025	0.0018	0.0009
Food manufacturing industries	5	0.0002	0.0001	0.0002
Beverage industries	6	0.0000	0.0000	0.0000
Tobacco manufactures	7	0.0000	0.0000	0.0000
Manufacture of textiles	8	0.0020	0.0020	0.0048
Manufacture of footwear, other wearing apparel, and made-up textile goods	9	0.0000	0.0000	0.0019
Manufacture of wood and cork, except manufacture of furniture	10	0.0055	0.0030	0.0020
Manufacture of furniture and fixtures	11	0.0008	0.0005	0.0003
Manufacture of paper and paper products	12	0.0067	0.0047	0.0021
Printing, publishing, and allied industries	13	0.0101	0.0026	0.0019
Manufacture of leather and leather products, except footwear	14	0.0003	0.0002	0.0003
Manufacture of rubber products	15	0.0165	0.0196	0.0004
Manufacture of chemicals and chemical products	16	0.0042	0.0031	0.0036
Manufacture of products of petroleum and asphalt	17	0.0042	0.0038	0.0002
Manufacture of nonmetallic mineral products	18	0.0017	0.0009	0.0014
Basic metal industries	19	0.0220	0.0168	0.0075
Manufacture of metal products, except machinery and transport equipment	20	0.0087	0.0066	0.0030
Manufacture of machinery, except electrical machinery	21	0.0149	0.0114	0.0058
Manufacture of electrical machinery, apparatus, appliances, and supplies	22	0.0201	0.0154	0.0074
Manufacture of transport equipment	23	0.2130	0.1651	0.0638
Miscellaneous industries	24	0.0003	0.0002	0.0002
House construction	25	0.0111	0.0042	0.0022
Other construction and work	26	0.0025	0.0016	0.0128
Electricity, gas, steam, and water services	27	0.0372	0.0077	0.0049
Trade	28	0.0347	0.0512	0.0040
Banking and insurance	29	0.0401	0.0220	0.0381
Railway transport	30	0.0087	0.0097	0.0051
Tramway and bus transport	31	1.0004	0.0002	0.0006
Other road transport	32	0.0245	1.0282	0.0081
Water transport	33	0.0090	0.0052	1.0312
Air transport	34	0.0000	0.0000	0.0001
Services incidental to transport	35	0.0004	0.0003	0.0045
Communication	36	0.0064	0.0042	0.0155
Central government	37	0.0003	0.0002	0.0035
Local authorities	38	0.0001	0.0001	0.0000
Other services	39	0.0063	0.0021	0.0033

Air transport	Services incidental to transp.	Communication	Central government	Local authorities	Other services
34	35	36	37	38	39
0.0015	0.0033	0.0016	0.0172	0.0532	0.0077
0.0000	0.0000	0.0000	0.0000	0.0001	0.0000
0.0070	0.0238	0.0095	0.0208	0.0218	0.0560
0.0030	0.0010	0.0024	0.0035	0.0023	0.0061
0.0006	0.0002	0.0002	0.0211	0.0384	0.0006
0.0001	0.0000	0.0000	0.0018	0.0026	0.0000
0.0000	0.0000	0.0000	0.0000	0.0000	0.0000
0.0013	0.0004	0.0003	0.0031	0.0054	0.0003
0.0001	0.0001	0.0000	0.0029	0.0067	0.0000
0.0056	0.0020	0.0058	0.0131	0.0092	0.0135
0.0010	0.0006	0.0016	0.0140	0.0117	0.0028
0.0061	0.0102	0.0046	0.0149	0.0148	0.0162
0.0101	0.0208	0.0062	0.0144	0.0211	0.0154
0.0004	0.0001	0.0000	0.0006	0.0010	0.0000
0.0017	0.0015	0.0008	0.0015	0.0015	0.0004
0.0052	0.0016	0.0032	0.0093	0.0061	0.0058
0.0003	0.0004	0.0006	0.0013	0.0005	0.0005
0.0016	0.0014	0.0064	0.0131	0.0102	0.0079
0.0329	0.0036	0.0150	0.0137	0.0101	0.0052
0.0128	0.0016	0.0048	0.0093	0.0071	0.0034
0.0224	0.0025	0.0097	0.0113	0.0096	0.0031
0.0307	0.0042	0.0503	0.0137	0.0134	0.0048
0.3222	0.0252	0.0115	0.0152	0.0091	0.0040
0.0005	0.0002	0.0049	0.0046	0.0037	0.0016
0.0047	0.0084	0.0210	0.0329	0.0363	0.0765
0.0052	0.0071	0.0519	0.0976	0.0375	0.0031
0.0122	0.0109	0.0274	0.0300	0.0355	0.0608
0.0110	0.0205	0.0094	0.0234	0.0403	0.0236
0.0282	0.0258	0.0141	0.0132	0.0288	0.0766
0.0143	0.0478	0.0187	0.0088	0.0028	0.0052
0.0007	0.0008	0.0236	0.0006	0.0004	0.0007
0.0252	0.0730	0.0173	0.0310	0.0246	0.0131
0.0052	0.0278	0.0023	0.0018	0.0017	0.0026
1.0002	0.0145	0.0005	0.0000	0.0000	0.0000
0.0115	1.0003	0.0002	0.0002	0.0002	0.0003
0.0232	0.0269	1.0175	0.0237	0.0100	0.0089
0.0222	0.0005	0.0006	1.0002	0.0058	0.0004
0.0001	0.0000	0.0000	0.0001	1.0001	0.0000
0.0083	0.0168	0.0089	0.0112	0.0110	1.0215

Bibliography

BIBLIOGRAPHY

AAROW, KENNETH J., AND HOFFENBERG, MARVIN. *A Time Series Analysis of Interindustry Demands.* Amsterdam: North-Holland Publishing Company, 1959.

AMES, EDWARD. "Linear Economics." Unpublished manuscript, Purdue University Department of Economics, Lafayette, Indiana, 1962.

ANGELL, JAMES W. *The Recovery of Germany.* New Haven: Yale University Press, 1929.

ARENDT, HANNAH. "Eichmann in Jerusalem—IV," *New Yorker* (March 9, 1963), p. 68.

AUER, JAAKKO. *Suomen Sotakorvaustoimitukset Neuvostoliitolle,* Porvo: Kirja Paino, 1956.

BANK OF FINLAND INSTITUTE FOR ECONOMIC RESEARCH (ed.). *Bank of Finland Monthly Bulletin,* XXVII, Nos. 7, 8, 9, 10 (1953).

BARNA, TIBOR. *The Structural Interdependence of the Economy, Proceedings of an International Conference on Input-Output Analysis.* New York: John Wiley and Sons, Inc., 1954.

BERGMAN, CARL. *The History of Reparations.* Boston and New York: Houghton Mifflin Company, 1927.

BRESCIANI-TURRONI, COSTANTINO. *The Economics of Inflation, A Study of Currency Depreciation in Post-War Germany.* London: George Allen and Unwin, Ltd., 1937.

BROWNLEE, K. A. *Statistical Theory and Methodology in Science and Engineering.* New York: John Wiley and Sons, Inc., 1960.

BURNETT, PHILIP MASON. *Reparations at the Paris Peace Conference From the Standpoint of the American Delegation,* Vols. I and II. New York: Columbia University Press, 1940.

BYRNES, JAMES F. *Speaking Frankly.* New York: Harper and Brothers, 1947.

CAMERON, BURGESS. "The Labor Theory of Value in Leontief Models," *Economic Journal,* LXII (March, 1952), pp. 191–94.

CHENERY, HOLLIS B., AND CLARK, PAUL G. *Interindustry Economics,* New York: John Wiley and Sons, Inc., 1959.

CHENERY, HOLLIS B., CLARK, PAUL G., AND PINNA, VERA CAO. *The Structure and Growth of the Italian Economy.* Rome: 1953.

CONDLIFFE, J. B. *The Commerce of Nations.* New York: W. W. Norton and Company, Inc., 1950.

DORFMAN, ROBERT. "The Nature and Significance of Input-Output," *Review of Economics and Statistics,* XXXVI, No. 2 (May, 1954), pp. 121–33.

DORFMAN, ROBERT, SAMUELSON, PAUL A., AND SOLOW, ROBERT M. *Linear Programming.* New York: McGraw-Hill Book Company, Inc., 1958.

EVANS, W. DUANE. "The Effects of Structural Matrix Errors on Interindustry Relations Estimates," *Econometrica,* Vol. 22, No. 4 (October, 1954), pp. 461–80.

EVANS, W. DUANE, AND HOFFENBERG, MARVIN. "The Interindustry Relations Study for 1947," *Review of Economics and Statistics,* XXXIV, No. 2 (May, 1952), pp. 97–144.

FORSSELL, OSMO, AND GRÖNLUND, PAAVO. *Panos-Tuotos-Tutkimus Suomen Talouselämästä Vuonna 1956* (Input-Output Study for Finland in 1956). Helsinki: 1960.

——— "Panos-tuotos-menetelma," *Kansan-Taloudellinen Aikakauskirja* ("Input-Output Method," *Finnish Economic Journal)* (1960), pp. 67–99.

——— Letters received dated October 10, 1962, and March 3, 1963, containing information from the Central Statistical Office of Finland.

FRASER, D. A. S. *Nonparametric Methods in Statistics.* New York: John Wiley and Sons, Inc., 1959.

GANTMACHER, F. R. *The Theory of Matrices,* Vol. 2. New York: Chelsea Publishing Company, 1959.

GEORGESCU-ROEGEN, NICHOLAS. "Leontief's System in the Light of Recent Results," *Review of Economics and Statistics,* XXXII, No. 3 (August, 1950), pp. 214–22.

HADLEY, G. *Linear Algebra.* Reading, Mass.: Addison-Wesley Publishing Company, Inc., 1961.

HOEL, PAUL G. *Introduction to Mathematical Statistics.* 2d ed. New York: John Wiley and Sons, Inc., 1958.

HOWARD, JOHN B. *The Paris Agreement on Reparations from Germany.* U.S. Department of State Publication No. 2584, European Series 12, 1946.

HURWICZ, LEONID. "Input-Output Analysis and Economic Structure, A Review Article," *American Economic Review,* XLV, No. 1 (September, 1955), pp. 626–36.

INSTITUTE OF ECONOMIC RESEARCH. *Theory and Application of Inter-industry Analysis.* Economic Research Series 4. Japan: Hitotsubashi University, 1961.

J. J. H. "Finland's Reparations," *World Today, New Series,* Vol. 8 (July, 1952), pp. 307–14.

JACKSON, J. HAMPDEN. "Finland Since the Armistice," *International Affairs,* XXIV, No. 4 (October, 1948), pp. 505–14.

JOHANSEN, LEIF. *A Multi-Sectoral Study of Economic Growth.* Amsterdam: North-Holland Publishing Company, 1960.

KEYNES, JOHN MAYNARD. *The Economic Consequences of the Peace.* New York: Harcourt, Brace and Company, 1920.

——— *A Revision of the Treaty, Being a Sequel to the Economic Consequences of the Peace.* New York: Harcourt, Brace and Company, 1922.

——— "The German Transfer Problem," *Economic Journal,* XXXIX (March, 1929), pp. 1–7.

KINDLEBERGER, CHARLES P. *International Economics,* Rev. ed. Homewood, Illinois: Richard D. Irwin, Inc., 1958.

KOOPMANS, TJALLING C. (ed.). *Activity Analysis of Production and Allocation. Proceedings of a Conference.* New York: John Wiley and Sons, Inc., 1951.

LEONTIEF, WASSILY. "Input-Output Analysis and Its Use in Peace and War Economics; Recent Developments in the Study of Inter-industrial Relations," *American Economic Review,* XXXIX, No. 3 (May, 1949), pp. 211–25.

——— "Some Basic Problems of Structural Analysis," *Review of Economics and Statistics,* XXXIV, No. 1 (February, 1952), pp. 1–9.

LEONTIEF, WASSILY, ET AL. *Studies in the Structure of the American Economy, Theoretical and Empirical Explorations in Input-Output Analysis.* New York: Oxford University Press, 1953.

LICHTENBERGER, HENRI. *Relations Between France and Germany.* Carnegie Endowment for International Peace and Education, No. 18. Washington, D.C.: 1923.

LINDGREN, BERNARD W. *Statistical Theory.* New York: The Macmillan Company, 1962.

MANTOUX, ETIENNE. *The Carthaginian Peace, or the Economic Consequences of Mr. Keynes.* London: Oxford University Press, 1946.

MEAD, W. R. "The Finnish Outlook . . . East and West," *Geographical Journal.* CXIII (June, 1949), p. 9.

MORISHIMA, MICHIO. "Prices, Interest and Profits in a Dynamic Leontief System," *Econometrica,* Vol. 26, No. 3 (July, 1958), pp. 358–80.

MORGENSTERN, OSKAR (ed.). *Economic Activity Analysis.* New York: John Wiley and Sons, Inc., 1959.

MOULTON, HAROLD G. (ed.). *The Reparation Plan.* New York: McGraw-Hill Book Company, 1924.

NETHERLANDS ECONOMIC INSTITUTE (ed.). *Input-Output Relations.* Leiden: H. E. Stenfert Kroese, N. W., 1953.

OHLIN, BERTIL. "The Reparation Problem: A Discussion," *Economic Journal,* XXXIX (June, 1929), pp. 172–73.

RASMUSSEN, P. NORREGAARD. *Studies in Inter-Sectoral Relations.* Amsterdam: North-Holland Publishing Company, 1957.

RYAN, JOHN M. "The Leontief System," *Southern Economic Journal,* XIX, No. 4 (April, 1953), pp. 481–93.

SHERWOOD, ROBERT E. *Roosevelt and Hopkins, An Intimate History.* New York: Harper and Brothers, 1948.

SIEGEL, SIDNEY. *Nonparametric Statistics for the Behavioral Sciences.* New York: McGraw-Hill Book Company, 1956.

TILASTOLLINEN PÄÄTOIMISTO. *Tilastokatsauksia,* Tammikuu 1955, XXX, No. 1, Helsinki: Bulletin of Statistics issued by the Central Statistical Office of Finland (January, 1955).

——— *Tilastokatsauksia,* Tammi-Helmikuu, 1950, XXV, No. 1–2, Helsinki: Bulletin of Statistics issued by the Central Statistical Office of Finland (January-February, 1950).

——— *Tilastokastauksia,* XXXVI, No. 1, 1961, Helsinki: Bulletin of Statistics issued by the Central Statistical Office of Finland (1951).

TOIVOLA, URHO (ed.). *The Finland Year Book 1947.* Helsinki: Mercatorin Kirjapaino ja Kustannus Oy, 1947.

UNITED NATIONS. *International Standard Industrial Classification of all Economic Activities.* Statistical Papers Series M, No. 4, Rev. 1. 1958.

U.S. DEPARTMENT OF STATE. *Treaties of Peace with Italy, Bulgaria, Hungary, Romania, and Finland.* No. 2744, Washington, D.C.: U.S. Government Printing Office, 1947.

——— *Making the Peace Treaties, 1941–1947.* No. 2774. European Series 24. Washington, D.C.: U.S. Government Printing Office, February, 1947.

——— *Paris Peace Conference, 1946.* No. 2868. Washington, D.C.: U.S. Government Printing Office, 1947.

——— *Foreign Relations of the United States* (Conferences at Cairo and Tehran). No. 7187. Washington, D.C.: U.S. Government Printing Office, 1961.

——— *Foreign Relations of the United States* (Conference of Berlin, the Potsdam Conference). No. 7015, Vols. I and II. Washington, D.C.: U.S. Government Printing Office, 1960.

VINER, JACOB. *Studies in the Theory of International Trade.* New York: Harper and Brothers, 1937.

WALRAS, L. *Elements of Pure Economics*. Homewood, Illinois: Richard D. Irwin, Inc., 1954.

WHITE, HARRY D. *The French International Accounts 1880–1913*. Cambridge: Harvard University Press, 1933.

WILLIAMS, JOHN H. *Post-War Monetary Plans and Other Essays*. Oxford: Basil Blackwell, 1949.

YOUNG, JOHN PARKI. *The International Economy*. New York: The Ronald Press Company, 1942.

ZARNOWITZ, VICTOR. "Technology and the Price Structure in General Equilibrium Systems," *Review of Economic Studies*, XXIII, No. 61 (1955–56), pp. 109–25.

Index

INDEX